Winni *Your Head*

A Complete Mental Training Guide for Soccer

Rafi Srebro

Translated from Hebrew by Vladimir Petcov

**Library of Congress
Cataloging - in - Publication Data**

by Rafi Srebro
    Winning With Your Head
        A Complete Mental Training
        Guide for Soccer

ISBN No. 1-59164-030-X
Lib. of Congress Catalog No. 2002110230
© 2002

Editing
Bryan R. Beaver

Printed by
DATA REPRODUCTIONS
Auburn, Michigan

Reedswain Publishing
612 Pughtown Road
Spring City, PA 19475
800.331.5191
www.reedswain.com
info@reedswain.com

This book is dedicated to my mother, my wife Edit and to my sons Gil and Ron who stood by my side during all the years of my studies and in loving memory of my father.

This book is dedicated to my mother, my wife Edit and to my
sons Gil and Ron who stood by my side during all the years
of my studies and in loving memory of my father.
Special thanks to coach Viki Hadad and to Professor Amir
Ben Porat for introducing me to the exciting field of sport
psychology and for contributing to the book.
Thanks to Professor Michael Bar-Eli, Dr. Zvia Sar-El Eker
and Michal Yaaron for reading the manuscript,
giving their remarks and thoughts and contributing
to the final design of the book.

Contents – Training Program

21 Steps for improving your mental abilities

Step 1   Be aware that your personal performance on the field is influenced by mental factors.

Step 2   Understand that mental abilities have important influence on the quality of your game.

Step 3   Stress is a normal reaction. See stress as a challenge not a threat.

Step 4   Use relaxations and breathe control.

Step 5   Use the power of visualization.

Step 6   Control Your Thoughts.

Step 7   Change your negative thoughts into positive.

Step 8   Use your mind in preparation for the game and during the game.

Step 9   Monitor your personal stress level and regulate it to best fit your abilities.

Step 10   Execute your personal and team roles.

Step 11   Take personal responsibility for the motivational level best suited to your potential.

Step 12   Define the right goals.

Step 13   Improve your self-confidence and believe in your abilities.

Step 14   Emotional control: play soccer with your legs and head, not with your emotions.

Step 15   Improve your concentration.

Step 16   Cope with injuries.

Step 17   Balance between fitness and mental strength.

Step 18   Rest is part of fitness training.

Step 19   Nutrition-You kick and run with what you eat.

Step 20 Exploit special game conditions.

Step 21 Persistence.

YOU CAN' T CUT IT SHORT! IF YOU DON'T PRACTICE YOUR MENTAL SKILLS DURING THE WHOLE SEASON, INVESTING IN MENTAL WORK ONLY BEFORE A MAJOR GAME WON'T HELP YOU!

Chapter 1 –Introduction - Long before the whistle

The idea to write this book existed inside my head for a long time. I decided to write it during the World Cup Games in France 1998, watching how game after game the best of players and teams in the world showed at times poor game mental performance and were unable to reach their full personal and team potential.

A good example was Brazil in the final. After the game we read what happened to the team and to Ronaldo (mental and physical breakdown). In the game we saw the influence of these events on the player and on the whole team. We saw a much lower personal and team performance in this game compared to the performance in the rest of the Championship.

I finished writing the book together with the end of EURO 2000. We saw at these games missed penalties, defender mistakes, goals at the last minutes of the game and lost goal opportunities. These examples are only a small part of the whole influence of **mental factors** on the game. The book in English will be published after the end of World Cup games 2002 in Korea and Japan. In the early rounds we saw again that not the teams with the most talented players won the games. Some of the most talented players and teams went home early - Argentina, France and Portugal. **In soccer like in any sport you need more than talent to succeed:**

**You need the mental ability to play
to your best in the most important game.**

The success of teams like Korea, USA and Turkey was attributed by their coach's and commentators to the mental toughness of those teams.

I write this chapter just after the final game of world cup 2002. Brazil wins the game and they are world champions. I mention Ronaldo in this chapter and latter in the book in connection to his level of play in 1998 world cup, Brazil lost and Ronaldo played one of the worst games of his career. We saw Ronaldo in world cup 2002, scoring 8 goals in 7 games including 2 goals in the final and becoming the top scorer of the tournament and one of the best players of world cup 2002.

Ronaldo's talent did not change during these 4 years, what changed was his mental ability. 4 years ago Ronaldo could not deal with the pressure and stress but throughout the 7 games we saw a different Ronaldo playing to his best .
The difference was his mental toughness that let him to play to his best!!!

What are the mental factors?
For the purpose of this book I define mental factors as:
Everything that happens in the mind/head of players.

Almost after every championship it is easy to find in the press quotations from players, coaches and commentators telling: "We were not mentally prepared", "The players were not mentally ready for the game" and many more related citations.
From my experience with soccer players, I have learned that most of the people involved with this sport have no idea what are the mental elements of the game.

The purpose of this book is to present to the reader in the following chapters, the mental factors involved in soccer, to analyze their influence and to learn how to practice and master them.

You score only some goals with your head but you always win or lose with your head!

At the end of the book a weekly mental training program is presented. In order to gain the maximum out of it, you should first read the book from beginning to end and only after this you may start working through the program.

After game 7 of 2002 NBA semifinal between Sacramento Kings and the Los Angels Lakers a reporter spoke about the Lakers preparation for the game. **In the morning before the game the team worked with a sport psychologist on relaxation and visualization**!! Those are two of the techniques you will learn in this book.

If some of the best players in the world use these techniques to prepare mentally for a game -You can use them too!

Chapter 2 - Who's in the team?
(To whom is this book relevant)

The book is intended for soccer players and coaches alike at all levels and age, and to every body who is involved and loves soccer: commentators, referees, journalists, soccer fans and more.

Experienced coaches and amateurs, professional players and just beginners, everybody in his field will find in this book issues that are of interest to him/her. Even more: this book offers a training program aimed at improving achievement and abilities in every aspects of life: Work, Study, Health and Sport.

<u>My Promise</u>: If you adopt even only a small part of the ideas of this book, you will be able to improve your abilities in every field.

If you are a player – you will become a better player

If you are a coach - you will be a better coach

If you are a referee – you will be a better referee

If you are a reporter or commentator – you will be better

If you are the owner of a team – you will be better

If you are the manager or a member on the board of a team – you will be better

If you only love the game – you will become a better fan

In the book I relate to the reader as a player, but as I already said the book is intended for everybody in the field, to women and men alike.

At the end of each chapter there is a summary. Read the chapter closely, go through the summary and try to think how it relates to you.

In addition, in every chapter there is "A coach box". It refers not only to coaches, it is important to everyone. Do not skip it!

The 21 steps that will lead you to improved personal ability follow along the book. It is important to refer to them in the context of the chapter in which they appear.

When you reach a Step, read it carefully think it over and try to check what it means to you.

If you treat reading this book as a practice - then it will provide you with training that will be of greatest benefit for improving your abilities.

Chapter 3 – The Training Program

I suggest you read this book at least twice. The first time is intended to help you build a general idea about the different topics in the book and the second reading will make you relate personally to the ideas of the book. At this stage, you should check how the topics are connected to what you do and to find for yourself what you are ready to adopt and with what you do not agree.

The real work starts after reading the book!

In order to be a better player you have to adapt the ideas of the book and incorporate them to your training schedule and to your regular activities in such a way that they become an indispensable part of your training.

The last chapter of the book is a weekly training program. If you adopt it and work according to it for sufficient time – you will become a better player!

Since the program is intended for every player, read it carefully and try to fit it to your needs.

In any case, there is not even one sentence in this book that says "the one and only right thing to do is....." and it is not compulsory to accept it. Every player is encouraged to find his/her "right thing" about the different topics of the book.

The book is not a replacement for working with a sport psychologist. If you would like to advance even more in the mental elements of the game, the right way is to work closely with a sport psychologist personally or together with your team. The psychology of sport includes topics beyond the content of this book and they can be influential on your ability as well.

You don't have to suffer a personal or team breakdown in order to start to train mentally. The same way that you don't wait for problems in physical fitness to start working out.

At the Olympic Games in 1996 more than 20 sport psychologists worked with the American delegation. They worked with athletes in all the individual and team sports. The Americans athletes did not work with psychologists because they were "nuts" or because they were not good athletes. They did so out of understanding that mental training can only improve their achievements. Not surprisingly at the 2000 Olympic Games in Sidney there were psychologists with most of the delegations.

Chapter 4 – What is Mental Strength?

Let's start to climb up the steps that will lead you to improved personal performance. We have 21 steps to climb. 21 steps on the way to improving your abilities.

Step 1: *Your personal performance on the field is influenced by mental factors.*

When I named this book **"Winning with your Head"**, I did not intend to teach you how to butt with your head (although I will try to do this as well).

Winning with your head means to take advantage of it in order to become better players and better teams.

What are the mental elements of the game?

- **Thoughts**
- **Believes and Feelings**
- **Stress**
- **Concentration**
- **Self-confidence**
- **Emotional Control**
- **Planning**
- **Analysis**
- **Motivation**
- **And all the other things that happen in your mind**

To each and every element there is an influence on your game. To be Mentally Strong means to be able to control and regulate your mind and what happens inside it, in order to improve your ability.

The most evident sign of Mental Strength is consistency and stability in ability!

Mentally strong are not those players that have a "Lucky Day", **but the players that are able to show their best ability in game after game!**

From this point of view, every sportsman has two goals:

1. To show his/her abilities in a consistent manner.
2. To achieve the maximum of his/her abilities
   (or to be close to the maximum).

Achieving these two goals is not easy, however it is definitely possible. Mental Strength can be learned. It is possible to train and improve this ability.

Just a few of us were born mentally strong, however everyone can become mentally strong!

Here is a list of the additional qualities that are typical for a mentally strong player:

- he has strong self-motivation and does not need someone
  to push him/her. This motivation is internal and pushing forward.
- he comes to the game in order to win the game, and he is
  ready to invest everything in order to win.
- he knows how to distinguish between the score of the game
  (win or loss) and personal performance.
- he is ready to learn from his/her mistakes and knows how to
  face the criticism.
- he is positive, but realistic, keeping a positive approach to
  himself and the game. he does not give up and never
  loses hope.

- he is in control of his/her feelings.

- he plays with mind and feet alone. he does not play with emotions: anger, fear, etc.

A Mentally Strong player does not kick the ball with anger, does not invest in retaliation, does not go blind with glory and never feels hopeless in the middle of the game.

- he is always calm and stable especially in moments of pressure.

- **Pressure does not frighten him/her. It becomes an opportunity to show up his/her abilities. Pressure is a challenge for him/her.**

- he stays concentrated on the game. Nothing can distract him/her. Throughout the game he is focused on what is happening on the field.

- he is always vigorous and full of energy.

- he has high self-confidence.

- he has full believe in his/her potential.

- he has no excuses and takes full responsibility for his game.

- he shows his best ability in a consistent way every game.

The mentally strong player has the following characteristics as well:

1. he brings his/her mind to the game and does not *"leave it at home"* or in the changing room.

2. his mental work continues through the whole game, till the final whistle.

3. he knows that a game of soccer does not start with the referee's whistle.

4. he is aware that the next game starts right after the final whistle of the present game.

The preparation for next game starts immediately after the final whistle of the game (in practical terms it starts after a couple of hours).

<u>Summary</u>

- The first step on the way to become a better player is the understanding that your abilities are influenced by mental factors.
- Mental strength can be developed and trained.
- The expression of mental strength is consistent ability.
- Your goal is to play to your best ability in every game and every training

<u>The Coach Box</u>

Everything I wrote about the game concerns you too. As a coach, you have profound influence on your players and it is important to be aware of the influence of mental factors over their performance.

Your message to the players should clarify that they must work to develop their mental strength. At the same time, you have to work on your mental strength as a coach. Ask yourself if you have reached the peak of your potential as a coach. If the answer is negative, the book will show you the ways that will bring you to the best of your potential as a coach, **in every training session and in every game.**

The best of the soccer teams in the world work with sport psychologists. Brazil, France, Spain are only a few of the

teams that are known to work with psychologists. If it is good for them, then **for sure it is good for every team, every coach and every player.**

Chapter 5 – Entrance Exam

Like in every entrance to a new position (your duty is to be an active reader), we start with an entrance exam that is intended to show you where you stand, according to your ability to win with your head.

We can look on the player's ability on the field as a composite of four elements:

- The player's **talent.**
- The preparation and **physical** qualities of the player
- The mental preparation and **mental** abilities of the player
- The player's **skill**

The Ability on the Field =

Talent + Skill + Physical Ability + Mental Ability

When speaking about **Talent** I mean the potential that the player brings with himself from birth.

Skill is what the player has learned through practice, watching replays on the video and all the experience he has acquired during his career.

By **Physical Ability** is meant all the body characteristics (height, strength, etc.) and the fitness of the player.

Mental Ability is the level of preparedness for the game and the control over the mental elements (concentration, believing in your ability, self-confidence, coping with stress, emotional control, etc.)

Write down the percentage you think each of these elements (talent, skill, physical and mental abilities) contributes to the success of the player on the field (if you are involved in soccer: a coach, a referee, a player, etc. think about yourself. If not think about players you know).

Talent   ......%
Skill   ......%
Physical Ability ...... %
Mental Ability   ...... %

In this exam, there is no right answer! The only mistake, in my opinion, in the estimation of these elements, is the belief of some players that the most important element is the talent. **The players that give talent the most importance for their success, I believe are wrong!**

If this was right and talent was the most important element for the success of the player, then there should be no difference in the performance of the player from game to game or between game and training, because talent is given and does not change from game to game!

However in reality, we know that such a situation does not exist.

Against the opinion that talent contributes the most for success, a great number of sportsmen around the world from different fields claim that up to 90% of their success is a result of their mental abilities.

They believe that in the high professional levels of sport there is not a significant difference between the athletes in the other elements. Everyone is talented, professionally skilled and physically trained. **The only difference between these players is expressed in their mental preparation and mental strength.**

The mental strength that allows the player to show his best ability in a consistent way, even in the most important game, accounts for the difference between the players success.

Even if you do not agree with this opinion, we can give more or less the same weight to each of the four elements (talent, skill, physical and mental ability). That is to say, that each element has 25% weight for the success of the player on the field.

The practical conclusion should be that you have to invest an equal amount of time to work and train on every one of the four different elements.

Step 2: *Understand that mental abilities have important influence on the quality of your game.*

Therefore, you have to develop and train these abilities. Improving your mental abilities will have immediate effect on improving your abilities on the field.

How Does It Work?

Players and teams are occupied most of the time in developing personal and team skills and in improving body fitness. The result is that soccer players develop to their peak in skill and in fitness, but it is very difficult for them to continue in their development. This is a result of the very small amount of time that they invest in developing their mental skills. That is something to be improved. It means - In order to improve their ability on the field, the only thing they should do is to advance and develop their mental potential.

Any improvement, even the smallest in the mental abili-

ty, will have immediate results in improving their ability on the field.

Working on mental ability should be similar to physical training. The same way you continue to work on your fitness every day and each training session, you should persevere in your mental training.

Exactly like there is no situation in which you can tell yourself **"I have achieved the maximum of my physical abilities, I do not need to practice anymore"**, the same way you should address your mental abilities training. This practice should be indispensable of your training and should be done every day, in the preparation for every game, during the game and at its end and so on without a break.

How much´better you can become?

The answer to this question depends as well on your talent, fitness and skill. If Ronaldo (or any other player that you respect) is situated at the top of the scale of personal potential and you are a couple of levels below him, it does not mean that from the moment you start to work on your metal abilities you will reach his level. Even though, I can promise you that you will be able to climb at least one level or more on this scale. And it is possible that you may reach Ronaldo's level of potential as well (without a doubt, if Ronaldo has worked more on his mental abilities, he too could be a better player).

If you succeed in showing ability that is close to
your full potential in the better part of your
games, you have started to climb up
the steps of improvement!
Soccer players, professionals that earn millions
or young players – are only human beings!!!

What influences us as human beings has its influence on soccer players and usually in a stronger way, because of the physical and mental difficulty of the game.

If from this book you will accept only this approach, you have already advanced a big leap ahead. Even though it sounds too simple, most of the people involved with soccer and around it, have forgotten that they are only human beings. This problem gets even more complicated, because the players themselves have forgotten that they are only human as well and it is largely accepted amongst them that there is no need for special mental preparation. The only thing that is important to them is their belief that they are always capable of reaching their "full" ability. And all this without taking into account that the player has not slept during the night, has argued with his wife/girlfriend hours before the game, and is angry with his coach or the players of the team. According to this belief, all the factors above will not influence the player and if he feels pressured before the game, the moment he enters the soccer field all the pressure will be forgotten.

To illustrate what I mean let's return to the final game of the World Cup in France 1998 and to Ronaldo. The decision of the player to participate in the game and the coach's decision to let him play, despite the events that past over him in the hours before the game is an example for ignoring the fact that the player is only a person (from both the side of the player and from the side of the coach). Only from this point of view is it possible to understand his participation in the game and the expectation that he is capable of showing his regular potential.(remember he suffered a mental and physical breakdown the night before the game).

**Ronaldo is only human and
the results were seen on the field.**

Another example from a different sport comes from basketball. Everyone will agree that Michael Jordan in addition to all his strengths is one of the athletes with greatest mental endurance (remember that consistency is the major characteristic of mental strength). He recounts in a TV interview that in the home games of the Chicago Bulls, his wife and children always sat in the same seats. And it was difficult to him to concentrate on the game till he saw them seated (in other words even he had problems concentrating in preparation for the game when he was worried about his family).

After the win over Utah Jazz on the way to the sixth NBA Championship, he said to an interviewer that what he wants now is to be with his wife and family. But he did not bring them with him to Utah to watch his final career game, because he knew that their presence would disturb him and would not allow him to be focused on the game. These are his own words – not my interpretation and these are not words of a young player, but of a player at the peak of his mental potential.

Real mental strength comes from the acceptance that you are only a human being!!! You are neither Super-Man nor a Star, even if it is written in the papers. Real strength comes with your awareness of your weaknesses!!!

Stars shine only in the sky and even there they are arranged in groups!

As an athlete you work day after day on every muscle in your body, in order to develop them and to make them stronger. Only one muscle never receives the same amount of practice:

The "muscle" inside your head.

Let's think about our brain/mind as a muscle just for illustration and develop a complete training program for the "muscle" in our head!

If you think that you have more soccer in you than you show in some of your games, it is time to start practicing your mental abilities!

In the chapters of this book different topics related to mental strength will be present to you. With their help you will learn how to improve yourself in every one of them.

If you "play the game with me" from beginning to end – your success is guaranteed.

Since we are writing about a team sport, your personal success depends on your fellow players and the team. That is why I will emphasize in some of the chapters the team aspects of the game and how you as a single player can influence the team.

Summary
- We are all just human beings.
- Mental abilities have important influence on your performance on the field.
- In order to be mentally strong the first step is to understand your weaknesses.

- The training of mental strength should be
done in the same way as physical training.
- There are no magic solutions. There is
only hard work that brings results.
- Go with me to the end of this book, start
practicing and you will become a better
player.

The Coach Box

I would like you to adopt two things from this book:

**1. The full understanding and all its relevance
of the fact that players (and coaches) are only
human beings.**

If a player wants to be able to show consistency in his
games, he needs to develop his mental strength. In an
interview a coach was asked once how he copes with
players pressure/stress . He replied that he tells them "Get
out of the pressure!" and with this he solves the problem.

**You can't regulate pressure by order
even if you try very hard.
Without the right means –
this is mission impossible.**

**2. The real understanding and all its relevance is
that every player is a unique and different person.**
It is impossible to reach the maximum of the potential

of each and every player if you treat them as the same. It is true about their physical fitness and for sure it is valid for mental ability (the level of motivation that suits one player, can bring to another player a level of pressure that does not allow him to function normally).

These are the subjects this book deals with.

> **Players are only human and each of them is a unique person!**
> **Coaches are only human too and each of them is a unique being!**

Chapter 6 – Stress

Everybody involved with sport knows what stress is. However, it is somewhat difficult to find a simple and complete definition for stress. In psychology we can find concepts like: anxiety, pressure, arousal, fear that are part of stress or linked to stress. In this and the following chapters we will try to understand what is stress, we will examine its causes and we will try to learn how to cope with it.

The goal is to reach a state in which you can tell yourself "Right now I feel stressed!". This is the first and most essential step. After it you will be able to recognize when you are under stress. This will allow you to pass to the next step and learn how to  deal with stress. In this stage you will learn how to reach your maximum potential even when you are under stress. **I will not teach you how to dismiss stress – this is impossible. You will learn how to face stress and regulate it, how to perform to your full potential even when in a stressed situation.**

My definition of stress:
Stress is what you feel and react to in a threatening situation and in uncertainty.

The threatening situation can be real, like a car that suddenly appears in your lane, somebody attacking you or an opposing player running towards you in order to tackle you. Threatening situations can also be vague and unreal.

In sport most threatening situations are a result of our thoughts and they exist only in our imagination or mind.

For example, the following thoughts:
- What will happen if we lose the game?
- What if I play badly or get injured in the game?
- What if I don't play well and the coach takes me out of the line-up?
- And many more…

Stress can come suddenly and last a second (a sharp turn when driving) or it can be continuous, like in soccer throughout the whole season.

Stress can cause a bad feeling, however it can also be pleasant like the uneasiness before a first date.

Stress can be negative and can hurt our performance, but it can be positive as well and push us to better functioning (to train and prepare better for the game and try harder).

In sport as in soccer, there are no situations of real stress – a threat over our lives or over our well-being. **The only real threat is about being injured by an opponent playe**r, when he is wildly running towards you and trying to hurt you intentionally.

We create all the other stress situations in sport; their origin is in our thoughts, imagination and feelings.

One of the main characteristics of a soccer game and in sport is **<u>uncertainty</u>**

It does not matter against who you are playing, you can never know in advance what will be the final score and you don't know how good you will perform in the game.

Uncertainty amplifies Stress!

(if you know the score from the beginning, you won't feel under pressure)

It is difficult and almost impossible to cancel the feeling of real stress, but it is possible to cope with it in such a way that will lessen its influence as much as possible.

It is certainly possible to significantly reduce the level of stress that originates in the thoughts that occupy our head and it is possible to regulate the level of stress!

What happens in our minds is the following process: when our brain recognizes a real or imagined stressful situation, it prepares the body for immediate reaction. People are capable of reacting to stressful situations in one of two ways: **fight or flight**. In other words, when we face a threatening situation our brain commands our body to prepare immediately to fight the threat or to run from it. This is a survival reaction that dates from the primitive ages of civilization. Accordingly, when the ancient man came across a small animal, he prepared to fight it, but if the animal was bigger and stronger than he was, he preferred to run away.

In short: he ate or he was eaten!

When we react to a dangerous situation today - even unreal and based on our thoughts, our body reactions are the same as the instinct to survive: to fight or to flight.

However, as people and especially as sportsman we cannot run or fight. On the contrary, we have to remain in position in the game, and function under stressful situations. As sportsmen we need more than just function, we need to give our best performance and maximum ability, and it is not a simple task.

What happens in our body at times of stress?

As we said, the body automatically prepares for survival reaction. In this state, our glands release in our body various substances. One of them is adrenaline, whose function is to prepare the different body systems for functioning in an emergency.

What do we feel when it happens?

In our body – the blood pressure rises and the heart beat gets faster in order to provide more blood to the muscles, the sugar levels in the blood rise as well providing more energy for muscle functioning. The body perspiration increases, in order to cool down the body and all the body systems that are not essential for survival stop or decrease their functioning (the digestive system and others).

Our emotions – there is a felling of danger
and anxiety

Our behavior – typical reactions are violence,
escape, withdrawal and lowering the reaction
threshold.

Our thoughts – it impairs our concentration ability,
we experience difficulty taking decisions
and confusion.

**All these changes find their expression in the body
and thoughts of the soccer player.
If they happen before or during the game they hurt the
player's ability to play to the maximum of his
potential.**

How does stress influence the player's ability during the game?

Does any stress hurt performance?

The answer to the questions lies in the following illustration. We call it the **inverted U-curve** (we will encounter this curve a couple times in the book, because it describes many of the factors that influence your ability).

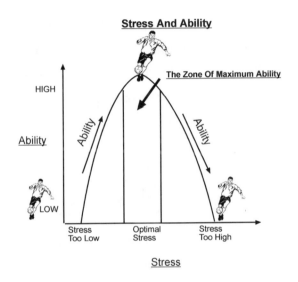

Stress And Ability

On the left side of the curve we can see that in the beginning **with the increase in stress levels our ability increases as well** until it reaches its maximum (an example for such a situation are contests or games without a crowd. In such games there is less stress and usually athletes and teams are unable to show their maximum ability). From this follows that a certain level of stress is essential. But still, **if stress level continues to rise, ability is impaired** (if we continue with the previous example, usually in big contests like the Olympics or the Finals of the World Cup, athletes do not break world records and the quality of the game is poor).

Each player has his own specific curve. In other words, the range of maximum ability changes from one player to another. Some players reach their maximum potential at lower stress levels, any increase in the level of stress will immediately impair their ability, and there are players that reach their maximum only under higher stress levels. Such players will be less influenced by great stress, however lower stress levels will lead them to poor performance.

Your goal: learn how you react to stress, so you can find the level of stress that best fits the range of your maximum potential. After you have achieved this, you should try to bring yourself to this level of stress, before and through the game.

This is not an easy goal – but it is certainly possible

This book will make it possible for you to reach this goal!

Let's check now how does stress express itself in athletes before and during the game.

<u>Signs of stress before the game:</u>

Some players can show signs of stress a couple of days before the game, and others can only feel the stress the night before the game or during the day of the game:

- Difficulty falling asleep.
- Difficulty to engage in activities that require concentration, like reading a book.
- Lower reaction threshold, being easily irritated by wife/friends/children.

- Lack of tolerance
- Difficulty remaining in the same place
- Stomach aches, feeling uneasiness in your stom ach, nausea, vomiting and diarrhea.
- Strong perspiration, frequent urination (everyone who has been in the dressing room before a game, has experienced the never-ending urge of the play ers to go to the rest rooms).
- Headache, dryness in the mouth.
- Cramp of muscles
- And any additional reactions that each of us has developed through the years.

The closer the day of the game gets, the stronger the feelings and signs of stress become.
Usually the peak level of stress is reached in the dressing room before the game.
Your personal feeling of stress and its signs get stronger the more the result of the game is important to you.

Although the list of stress signs is long enough, every player has his own typical signs of stress too. Certainly not every sign is present in all of us. Once I worked with a top player that was vomiting almost before every game and with another excellent player that was yawning exaggeratedly in times of stress. (Just think what his coach though about it half a hour before the game, while he was giving the last instructions - in front of him is sitting a player who is constantly yawning. In this case, I advised the player to talk personally with his coach and to explain to him that the yawns are result of the stress that he feels and not because he didn't sleep the night before the game).

There is only one way to know and recognize the signs of stress. Every player should be aware how he experiences stress and its intensity, and be able to say "Now I am under stress" or "I feel under more intense stress than usual".
Only the moment when you accept that you are under stress and you recognize its level of intensity, will you be able to deal with it.
From my personal experience and from the knowledge of others, we know that athletes prefer to deny the stress and not to recognize it.
Athletes treat stress as a personal weakness.

I met a player who was having diarrhea before every game. This player never connected this to stress. He always had a reasonable explanation for his situation (I ate something bad etc.).
The biggest mistake of a player is the denial of the stress he feels. This denial prevents him from dealing with stress and causes an immediate harm to his performance on the field.

Gaining stress awareness is the first step in coping with stress.

Read again through the list of stress signs and try to find which of them fits your reaction when you are under stress.

An additional mistake of many players and coaches is the belief that when you are on the field and the game begins the stress disappears.
This wrong conception is the reason why, even those

players that are conscious about the signs of stress, still don't do anything to cope with stress, because they are sure that with the entry to the field for warming up or later when the referee blows the whistle, the stress will disappear and they will play to their best.

This belief is completely wrong. Stress does not disappear on the field, it simply shows itself in a different way.

Usually, when players enter the game, the physical signs of stress disappear (there is no urge to go to the rest room, stomach aches disappear, etc.). This is because the body "knows" that there is no possibility right now to continue to go to the toilet, but it does not mean that stress has gone.

A player that was under stress in the changing room will continue to be under stress on the field as well.

Signs of stress on the field:

Lack of concentration – difficulty performing successfully even the simplest passes.

Mistake in perception – wrong calculation where the ball will go and mistakes in approach to the ball.

Violence – committing crude fouls

Low reaction threshold – easily getting angry, yelling, cursing etc. (usually yelling and cursing at the players on the same team over mistakes in their play etc.)

Coordination troubles – lack of coordination between the eye and the feet that hurts performance

Feeling of heaviness in the legs – even before the player has started to run, he already feels that its is hard to him to move around, his speed is lower and his flexibility is limited

Feeling tired – physical and mental exhaustion from the beginning of the game

Easily giving up – loosing hope and not trying harder

Tendency to run away from the game and not to cooperate – this finds its expression, when every time you try to pass the ball to another player he is already well guarded by a defender. Sometimes he even signals not to pass him the ball (a midfielder that doesn't come to fetch the ball). Sometimes you can see a tense forward that tries to hide himself behind the defender who is marking him. Looking from aside, you can see that not the defender follows the forward, but on the contrary, the forward attaches himself to the defender. In this way he can not receive the ball and nobody can criticize him afterwards. In many cases it's the forward that complains to the other players that they don't pass him the ball.

Difficulties breathing and dryness in the mouth - feeling of lack of air, that is felt not at the end of the game, but even before the first sprint - the air is gone.

These signs of stress change from player to player and not all of them appear in all the players. Specific signs of stress develop in every player during his career. It is understandable, that the appearance of a part of these signs in the players, even for a short period of time, hurts their performance and leads them to making mistakes.

It is important to recognize the signs of stress that are typical for you. This way if you were unable to cope with the stress before the game you will be able to deal with it throughout the game.

This is a more difficult task, but it is still possible!

Read through the list of stress signs on the field again and try to understand in what way they appear in you.

Some of the players are ready to admit that they enter the field tense. However, they are wrong when thinking that this is not a big problem, because after a couple of minutes in the game they already get rid of the stress and succeed in showing their maximum ability.

Sometimes this is true. The tension can disappear after a couple of minutes, but what will happen in these minutes, until the stress is gone? When we are dealing with professional sport we don't have the opportunity to play poorly in the first minute of the game and then to improve our play. Sometimes you won't be able to correct the first 5 minutes of lack of concentration with 85 minutes of excellent game.

Mistakes you make in the first five minutes of the game, can be the difference between winning and losing!

Everyone who is interested in soccer knows that many goals and missed goal opportunities happen in the first five minutes of the game, and usually the reason for this is lack of concentration as a result of tension in the players.

The main aim of every player (in order to show his maximum ability from the first whistle to the end of the game), should be the **recognition of his feeling of stress and its intensity <u>before</u> a game, and the ability to handle these   feelings before he enters the field.**

The secondary goal should be to correctly and immediately identify the feelings of stress and their intensity in a player <u>**during**</u> the game. In this way the player will be able to deal with this feelings or (not less important) can change his game to fit the existing situation.

<u>*Step 3*</u>*: Stress is a normal reaction but it is necessary to control it!*

In this step you should achieve:

- The right recognition of stress
- Estimation of the stress intensity
- Regulation of the level of stress to the most suitable
  level in order to best fit your maximum potential

After you gain an understanding about the signs of stress and you admit that the denial of stress is a mistake, you will learn how to cope with stress before the game and till the final whistle.

Your goal should be to deal with stress before the game, so when you enter the stadium, you will be able to fit your level of stress to your best game potential (accordingly to the curve we saw earlier).

The ability to cope with stress during the game is a lot smaller compared to the ability to do so before the game. It is important to leave the unnecessary stress at home or in the dressing room.

Before you learn how to cope with stress, it is important to learn what your stress level is at a certain time and what is the stress level that you need in order to reach your maximum potential.

To achieve this I offer you to build for yourself a stress-meter. It can be much like the speedometer of a car or like a digital meter or like scales or any other measure that fits. Now, concentrate on the stress signs that happen in you in this moment (your breathing rate, stomachaches, uneasiness, inner turmoil, lack of concentration, etc.) and try to give them a number value from one to ten.

Do this now!

This value in fact indicates the level of stress when reading this book (I hope its low).

Now, try to close your eyes and remember your last game. Go back with your imagination to the dressing room and try to think of a number that will describe the level of stress that you experienced before the game.

Do this now!

Close your eyes again and try to remember your best performance - the game in which you felt you reached the maximum of your potential. Try to remember how you felt before the game and write down according to your stress-scale the level of stress you experienced before the game.

Do this now!

The three different values express your stress level at the moment, the stress level you experienced before your last game and the level of stress you need in order to reach your maximum performance.

What is left for you to learn, right now, is how to control your stress level and always reach the best suitable stress level for your maximum performance on the field. This is what we will do next. Meanwhile, try to train yourself to work in different situations with your stress meter. Give yourself a stress value that describes the level of stress you experience the night and the morning before the game, couple of hours before entering the field, in the changing room, while warming up on the field, with the blowing of the referee's whistle and in other situations throughout the game.

In your free time try to train and find the level of stress you need in order to achieve your maximum ability. You have had for sure a lot of good games. Try to remember them and remember the stress level you had before the game, till you reach the right value for achieving the maximum of your abilities. Be aware that we don't speak about one value but a range of values.

(For example: stress in rest 1 – 2, stress in the changing room before a game 8 – 9, the best suitable stress for your performance 6 – 7, etc.)

<u>Summary</u>

- Everyone feels tense to one level or another. Stress influences us all.
- Stress is not always a negative thing.

- It is important to learn how stress expresses itself in you.
- It is important to be able to recognize the level of stress you experience in every moment.
- A player under stress won't be able to reach his best performance.
- A player who feels tense in the changing room will be tense on the field as well. Stress does not disappear.
- Stress leads to lack of concentration and lack of concentration leads to mistakes.
- Stress makes it difficult for you to control your emotions. Loss of control over your feelings leads to mistakes and in many cases to a red card.
- It is important to know what is the stress level you need to achieve the maximum of your potential

The Coach Box

Too much stress is an enemy for your players and prevents them from becoming what they are. Stress does not disappear alone and it is your duty to require the players to learn how to regulate their tension. To make this possible, you should pass the facts and the techniques of this book to them.

Your responsibility as a coach is to ensure that your players have the right means to cope with stress and that they are exploiting them in the proper way.

Chapter 7 – Coping With Stress

When we ask players what is the major factor that prevents them from reaching their maximum ability, they speak about difficulty in dealing with the tension and pressure of the competition. With the exception of few players and exceptional individuals that are not influenced by stress (do not decide that you belong to those few, **you are not!**), **every other player must learn how to deal with stress.**

Every soccer player that has acquired professional skills has developed for himself a way to deal with stress. In this chapter I will present useful methods and some even may be new for you. **The objective is to find the methods that you will feel comfortable with and, based on them, develop for you a way to cope with stress**. Of course, this book does not claim to present all the methods to deal with stress. If you don't succeed in developing a successful way for coping with stress for yourself I sincerely advise you to turn to a sport psychologist in order to find together the suitable method for you.

Like every new skill, you will have to invest a sufficient amount of time in training and enough time to test the method. Try to use different methods and only after experiencing them all decide which one is most suitable for you.

How not to approach Stress
Drugs, Alcohol and Smoking

The need to function under stress places a heavy load over the players and some of them turn to an easy solution: different drugs, smoking and drinking alcohol.

In British soccer we hear from time to time about players that got addicted to drugs and alcohol. The same with the American basketball, almost every year players get caught while on drugs and are expelled from the league. These players are aware that if caught on drugs they will lose income of millions of dollars, and still their lack of ability to cope with stress leads them to turn to the seemingly easier solution.

Drugs and alcohol can give the illusion of lowering stress for a short time, but the damage that they cause is many times greater than their "benefits".

Don't be tempted by alcohol and drugs.

If the stress overwhelms you and does not allow you to function the way you want, consult a psychologist, exactly the same as when your leg hurts and you go to a physician.

The Causes of Stress

In sport the major source of stress is in you. We speak about the following factors:

- **Your thoughts**
- **Your feelings**
- **The things you say to yourself**
- **The explanation and definition you give to situations**

If you are the major source of stress, then stress can be under your control and there is a lot you can do.

It is true that in many cases external factors exist that put pressure on you:

- The coach – "This is an important game for you". This sentence is common in coaches that intend to encourage the player, however, it can lead to unnecessary stress.

- The management or the President of the team – "You have to win, otherwise the future of the club is in danger…" Another widespread sentence that is intended to encourage but can lead to stress.
- The Press and the Media– including reporters and commentators, fans, family and more.

All these are external factors that can increase stress, still what will lead to a significant increase of your tension is your personal interpretation of the situation.

What makes the stress is not what the others say, write, etc., but the way you interpret what they say, write, etc.
If you succeed in changing your thoughts,
you will change the
definition of the situation
and you will be able to control stress.

The goal that stands in front of you is to control stress and to regulate it to the most suitable level for reaching your best performance. In order to be able to complete this goal and to regulate the level of stress to the most suitable level for your performance, you should learn to control your stress level using the following methods:

- **Relaxation** – a technique for loosening up the mind and the body
- **Visualization** – the use of imagination as an instrument of mental work

- Control over your thoughts

- Planning and Analysis

In the following chapters I will offer you different approaches to these methods that will allow you to cope with stress.
The appropriate way to benefit from these methods is to integrate them into your sporting life-style.
After you experience different methods, you will learn to use together relaxation and visualization, positive thinking, planning and analysis. **This combination will enable you to achieve complete metal preparation**.

Summary

- Drugs, Alcohol and Smoking do not help you deal with stress
- The major cause of stress lies in the player himself
- It is possible to control the level of stress and to regulate it to fit your maximum ability
- Mental preparation includes: relaxation, visualization, thought control, planning and analysis

The Coach Box

Stress is the major factor that prevents players from showing their maximum ability in a consistent manner. As a team coach, you know your players. Some of them deal with stressful situations and others do not.

Stress hinders them all, even those who apparently manage to deal with stress. In the following chapters I will present to you methods and tools to deal with stress and regulate it.

When players are not trying to regulate stress, they are likely to be tempted to turn to the easier solutions. The use of drugs and alcohol is becoming more and more common. You have to be vigilant and to recognize as early as possible the behavioral changes that appear in your players and to act accordingly.

Chapter 8 – Relaxation

One of the ways to regulate stress is the use of relaxation and deep breathing.

Integrate these methods into your sports life!

The use of relaxation is recommended for everybody, especially to people who work under stress: players, coaches, executives, etc. Relaxing at least once a day is recommended without any connection to our feeling of stress. Relaxation is important especially when we feel under stress. The feeling we achieve after relaxing is much better.

You devote so much time training your muscles,

to train the "muscle" inside your head you need

only 12 minutes a day!

Different relaxation methods exist. Below are some simple and efficient exercises that can be combined with each other. The goal of all methods of relaxation is the same:

To clear the mind from thoughts and to relax the body.

As we saw, the source of stress lies in your head – in your thoughts and feelings. If you succeed in clearing your mind from the thoughts that overwhelm you, you will succeed in lowering your stress level.

Relaxation with deep breathing

This exercise is common to all the methods of relaxation. It is very simple for execution and can be performed in any place, even on the field during the game.

The aim of this exercise is to maximize the flow of oxygen to the brain and the body. The result will be a pleasant feeling and physical relaxation.

The exercise can be done while seated, lying or standing – in any situation.

In the beginning when you are still learning the exercise, my advice is to perform it sitting. When you perfect this technique, you will be able to perform it in any situation. Sit down comfortably and start to breathe slowly through the nose. Usually, we stop inhaling when our chest rises – inhale a couple of deep breaths and pay attention how your chest rises. Now try to continue to inhale after your chest has risen, till you feel that your stomach is full with air (the belly rises up). You should breathe without effort and your body should be relaxed. After you have reached the full capacity of your lungs, keep your breath for a couple of seconds and exhale the air slowly and constantly through the mouth till all the air is out.

You should reach a state in which the time you exhale the air is twice as long as the time it takes you to inhale it.

In order to carry out this exercise properly, read first how to perform it and only after this try to complete it:
- Sit down comfortably, close your eyes, put your hands on your stomach bellow the ribs, breathe a couple of regular breathes, relax your body and concentrate on your breathing
- Start inhaling slowly through your nose, while counting slowly (in your mind) from one to four. Feel your chest rise and continue breathing in till you feel your hands start to rise too with your belly

- Stop breathing in, hold your breath and count slowly from one to four.
- Breathe out through your mouth very slowly and continuaously. While you are exhaling the air count slowly from one to eight. When you reach eight all the air should be out of your lungs.

The whole exercise should be performed without effort.

- Repeat the exercise a couple of times. Pause after each breath and check that you perform the exercise correctly.
- Breathe 5 deep continuous breaths without any effort and with body relaxed. When finished, open your eyes and try to describe how you feel to yourself.

Closing your eyes is not necessary. You can breathe deeply with your eyes open as well. Placing the hands on the stomach (below the ribs) is not essential either. These are only essential conditions for learning the technique and are intended to show you how your stomach rises. When you acquire this skill, you won't need to put your hands on the belly.

How did you feel after the breaths?

Usually you experience a pleasant feeling. May be you felt a bit of dizziness. This is a normal reaction and it will disappear with exercising.

Perform deep breathes in the following days on different occasions. In any case, breathe at least once a day five deep continuous breaths.

Remember that this is a new exercise for you, you have to practice it in order to become skillful with it.

Relaxation with counting your breath

The goal is to practice relaxation at least 12 minutes once a day (desirable twice a day).

Read twice through the following instructions and afterwards try to perform them:

- Sit down or lie comfortably on a place that is not very different from the conditions of the changing room, because later you will want to relax with this exercise before a game. Ask that you are not to be disturbed while practicing the exercise. If during the exercise you have to change your position or scratch your nose, do so. Loosen up tight clothes. Don't cross your legs or your hands, so that they don't put unnecessary tension on your body.
- Close your eyes and concentrate on your breath. Feel the air enter and exit your body. Concentrate for a couple of seconds on your breath alone.
- With your mind go through all the parts of your body, from the head to the feet and check that all your limbs are relaxed and nothing makes you tense. Feel your head and neck relaxed, your eyes closed in rest, so too your face, hands, stomach and feet. Concentrate on your breath. Adopt a passive attitude about what is happening around you. Ignore the different noises and the thoughts that rise inside your mind during the exercise. Put them aside. Don't deal with them and don't try to fight them. Concentrate only on your breath – a quiet and calm breath. Now, when your mind is clear from thoughts, very slowly in your own rhythm inhale 5 deep breaths. You can breathe them continuously or take a regular breath between the deep breaths. Do this exercise very slowly.

Letting the air out, you feel how the pressure and tension disappear.

- Concentrate again on your regular breathing. Your breath now is slower and calmer than before. Start counting your breaths. With every breath out, add a number in your mind and continue till you reach the number 10. When you reach 10 breaths, start counting again from one.
- Breathe a couple of series of 10 regular breaths (The only reason for counting the breaths is to prevent your mind from being occupied with thoughts. The best sign that thoughts are always trying to enter your mind is the confusion when counting. When it happens, concentrate on the counting and leave your thoughts aside). Performing the exercise you feel your body become more and more relaxed, your hands become heavy and a pleasant feeling of tiredness comes over you. Your mind is clean from thoughts and you concentrate only on counting your breaths.
- When you decide to finish the exercise, do this gradually. If you want to go to sleep this exercise will help you fall asleep quickly. At the end, you will be able with the help of your imagination to picture yourself in a beautiful and calm place. Try to concentrate on the details of this picture, the colors, the voices, the movement and you will fall asleep without a problem.

If after the end the exercise you return to regular activity, before you finish it, you should stop counting the breaths and concentrate on your breathing. In this state, breathe two deep breaths and concentrate again on your regular breathing.

- Start counting slowly from one to five. The more you advance in the count, the more energy you gain. You are full of vigor and power. You are prepared now for completing your tasks. You are certain now in your ability to finish them.

Open your eyes slowly, and don't stand up immediately. Give yourself a minute or two before your return to action, refreshed and full of energy.

Read the instructions of the exercise a couple of times and start training it once or twice a day. Don't be bothered by the time you invest in it, until you decide to finish it. The more you exercise, your body will find the amount of time it needs.

Don't try to fight with the clock. Keep your mind clean and maintain a passive attitude.

Perform this exercise a couple of times and see how pleasant it is!

If you have trouble giving yourself instructions during the exercise, you can prepare a tape with the instructions of the exercise.

<u>Summary of the basics of the exercise:</u>

Sit or lie comfortably.

Close your eyes.

Relax your body.

Adopt a passive attitude.

Breathe 5 deep breaths.

Concentrate on your breathing and count your breaths for a couple of minutes.

Breathe 2 deep breaths.

Return slowly from relaxation to regular functioning or fall asleep.

Relaxation with Deep Breathing

If you feel comfortable breathing deeply and you don't feel dizziness, you can perform the previous exercise. However, instead of breathing and counting your regular breaths you will have to perform and count deep breaths. This is exactly the same method and its principles are the same. Since when breathing deeply you do 3 – 4 breaths a minute, to complete a 10-minute exercise you have to perform 30 – 40 deep breaths.

Remember, this method is good only to those who don't have a problem with deep breathing!

Relaxation: contracting and releasing parts of the body.

Read the instructions of the exercise a couple of times then try to practice it by yourself.

We are still trying to achieve the same thing – clearing our mind of thoughts and relaxing the body.

Ask the people around you not to disturb you during the exercise.

If you need to change position during the exercise or to scratch yourself, do this.

- Lie or sit down comfortably. Close your eyes, concentrate on your breathing and be passive about the thoughts that occupy your mind.

Release tight clothes, don't cross your hands, fingers or legs, this will avoid unnecessary tension on the body.

Put your hands next to your body.

- Concentrate on your breathing and very slowly with your

own rhythm breathe 5 deep breaths like we learned earlier. When finished return to regular breathing.

- Concentrate only on your breathing.

- Close both your fists. Clench them tightly and concentrate on the unpleasant feeling of the tightness for a couple of seconds. Then, release the clench a bit and concentrate on the difference in the feeling.

  Now totally release your fists and feel how the tension and the unpleasant feeling are replaced with a feeling of comfort and relaxation. Concentrate carefully on the difference between the feeling of tension and the feeling of relaxation.

- Let's go to the arms. Stretch them strongly downward. Feel the tension in the muscles of your hands and keep them this way for a few seconds.

  Release the stretch a bit and experience the difference between the feeling of tension and the feeling of release. Remain this way for a few seconds and then release the stretch completely.

  Concentrate on the difference between the feeling of tension in your muscles and the feeling of relaxation.

  Concentrate on your relaxed hands and feel how the pressure and tension are replaced and a pleasant feeling of relaxation fills your body.

- Let's go to the feet. Distance your feet one from the other and stretch them strongly downward. Concentrate on the feeling of tension in your leg muscles and remain in this position for a couple of seconds.

  Release your feet slightly and try to feel the difference between the feeling of tension before and the loosening of your muscles now. Remain in this state for some seconds and then relax completely. Concentrate on the full relaxation of your feet and feel the tension and pressure disappear and the pleasant feeling of relaxation enter your body.

- Relax your hands and feet. A pleasant feeling of heaviness spreads through your limbs. Your breathing now is very quiet. Concentrate on this feeling of relaxation for a few seconds.

- Now tighten your stomach muscles and concentrate on the feeling of tension. Stay in this state for some seconds and then release your stomach muscles a bit . Concentrate on the feeling of slight release and keep this state for a couple of seconds. Now completely release your stomach muscles and feel how the feeling of relaxation spreads through your stomach and chest.
Concentrate on the difference between the feeling of tension and the feeling of relaxation. Your breathing now is very quiet.
A pleasant feeling of heaviness spreads through your body.
If thoughts enter your mind, don't fight them! Put them on the side.

- Now, raise your shoulders towards the head. Feel the tension in your muscles and remain in this state for some seconds then slightly lower your shoulders and feel the difference in the feeling. Remain this way for a few seconds and then release your shoulders completely. Let the feeling of relaxation spread through the muscles of your neck.

Concentrate on the feeling of relaxation that immerses your body. Feel your hands, feet, stomach, chest, shoulders and neck completely relaxed.

Concentrate deeply on the feeling of relaxation.

- Clench your jaws. Tightly close your mouth and feel the pressure. Stay this way for a few seconds and then release the clench a bit and feel the difference. Remain in state for a while and then completely release the mouth muscles. Concentrate now on the feeling of concentration.

- Close your eyes tightly and feel the feeling of pressure. Remain in this state for a few seconds, slightly release your face muscles and concentrate on the difference in the feeling. Remain in this state for a while then completely relax your eye muscles. Concentrate on the feeling of relaxation. Let it spread through all the muscles of your face: to the forehead, lips, jaws and cheeks.

Your entire body from the feet to the head is relaxed. A pleasant feeling spreads through your body. Concentrate only on your breath and feel the air enter and exit your body.

Remain it this state for some minutes.

- When you decide to finish the exercise, do this gradually. If you plan to go to sleep, this exercise will help you fall asleep easily. At the end of the exercise try to imagine a nice and calm scenery. Try to concentrate on the details of the picture: the colors, the voices and the movements.

If you plan to return to regular activity after the exercise, before the end of the exercise, concentrate only on your breathing and inhale two deep breaths.

Then, concentrate again on your regular breathing and start counting slowly from one to five. The more you advance in the count, the more your body gets full of energy. It gets full of vigor and strength.

Now, you are ready for the assignments that are waiting for you. You believe in your ability to complete them.

- Open your eyes very slowly and don't stand up immediately. Give yourself a minute or two more before you return to your daily activities, refreshed and full of power.

Read the instructions a couple of times and start training with it once or twice a day. Don't bother yourself with the amount of time it takes you to decide to finish it.

The more you practice; your body will find the most suitable amount of time for relaxation. Don't fight with time. Keep your mind clear and maintain a passive attitude. Practice this exercise and discover how pleasant it is.

After you perform the exercise a couple of times, try to fit it to your needs. You are able to concentrate on tightening and relaxing of all the muscles of your body or part of them according to your personal level of stress and taking into account the amount of time available.

Summary of the basics of the exercise:
Sit or lie comfortably.
Close your eyes.
Relax your body.
Adopt a passive attitude.

Breathe 5 deep breaths.

Concentrate on tightening and releasing body parts.

Experience the good feeling of a relaxed body.

Return slowly from relaxation to regular functioning or fall asleep.

Relaxation for young players

Actually, this exercise is **suitable for everybody**. If the previous exercises were not attractive for you, you can try this one instead.

Read the text a couple of times and then sit comfortably, close your eyes and perform the exercise following the instructions.(based on Orlick's Spaghetti Toes Relaxation Exercise [1]).

In this exercise you will try to talk to your body.
It sounds strange to you?

There is no problem talking to your body. Your body, amazingly enough, will actually do what you tell it to do.

- Tell the your toes to start moving! Check if they do.
- Tell the toes of your right foot to move alone! Check them out.
- Tell the toes of your left foot to move.
- Stop them.
- Now tell the toes of your feet to move very slowly, like in slow motion.
- Now, tell your toes to increase their speed… and after this command them to move slowly again… and to stop.

Your toes listened to your orders! Good! If you talk to parts of your body in the same way you talked to your toes, your body will listen to you and will perform your orders. Especially, if you perform them a number of times.

Let's learn now to talk to your body.

As a beginning lets think about chocolate.

I love chocolate the same as you and many others.

Chocolate that has been long in the fridge or in a cold room becomes hard and is easily broken.

On the contrary, when chocolate is left under the sun it becomes hot, soft and flexible, especially when it's wrapped on a plate.

- Let's try now to make your body hot, soft and sleepy like a hot piece of chocolate. Perhaps, we will need to talk a lot to the body until it understands exactly what we want from it. We will start from the toes. As a beginning we will work with the right foot. Tell the toes of your right foot to start moving very slowly and then tell them to stop. Command them to become hot and flexible like soft chocolate…! Repeat the same with the toes of your left foot. Tell them to remain this way.

- Now, move your right foot slowly…and then tell it to stop and become hot, flexible and sleepy like soft chocolate…

- Now move the left foot and tell it too to become hot, flexible and sleepy like hot chocolate. Your feet are hot and soft right now – hot and soft.

- Now move the fingers of your right hand very slowly… stop them and tell them to become hot, soft and sleepy…

- Now move the fingers of your left hand very slowly… stop them and tell them to become hot, soft and sleepy, like soft chocolate…

- Now move your right hand very slowly… stop it and tell it to become hot, soft and sleepy…

- Move your left hand too and tell it to become hot, soft and sleepy. Right now, your hands and fingers are hot, soft and sleepy.

- Try to tell your whole body to become hot…soft…and sleepy. Feel how your whole body heats up and becomes like hot and soft chocolate.
- Concentrate on your breath and tell it to be very, very quiet. Now your whole body is calm, hot, soft and sleepy… Remain in this state for a few minutes.
- When you decide that you want to stop, start counting very slowly from one to five. The more you advance with the count, the more your body will become full of energy, vigor and strength and will be ready for the assignments standing in front of you. You believe in your ability to complete them.
- Open your eyes very slowly and don't stand up immediat-e ely. Give yourself a minute or two more before you return to your daily activities, refreshed and full of power.

When can the chocolate exercise can help you?

When you are afraid or when you are under stress and your body is stiff like chocolate that comes out of the fridge. With your body like that, it is most certain that you won't succeed in showing your ability on the field. The chocolate exercise can be used suc-cessfully before you enter the field (or before you take an exam).

---

(1) Orlick, T.1992. Freeing children from stress:Focusing and stress control activities for children.ITA Publication.Willits. USA.

When you feel very tense, if you succeed in
relaxing the body and turning it soft and
at ease as a hot and soft chocolate,
you will be a better athlete.

In order that this exercise is successful, you have to practice it until you acquire the ability not to think about what is happening around you. You can command your body to perform the exercise. Start from your toes till you reach your final goal.

Summary

Relaxation is a technique. In order to perform it with success, it is necessary to train and practice it as much as possible. Don't expect immediate results and don't be discouraged if you don't succeed in performing the exercises or you don't feel the feelings mentioned in the text after the exercise. Instead, continue performing the exercise the best you can. Persistence will pay you back. The more skilled you will be in performing the exercise, the better you will feel at its end. You will be capable of reaching relaxation almost anywhere and in any state: at home, in the changing room before the game, in the bus on the way to the game, during halftime in the changing room (a short exercise), on the bench of reserve players and more.

- **It is important to learn and practice relaxation every day as a part of your soccer life.**
- **Choose a relaxation technique that suits you.**
- **Relaxation clears your mind from thoughts and helps you regulate stress.**
- **Deep breathing is a simple but very powerful technique. Breathe deeply at every occasion.**

The Coach Box

We already said that soccer players are only human beings and it is important that you too believe in this both about the players and about yourself.

Looking at your players you should be sensitive to their signs of stress away from the field and in the game. If you ignore the stress, it won't disappear. Your duty is to lead the players to their maximum personal and team performance and this requires mental training.

Don't try to be the psychologist of the team. It is impossible in your position as a coach. Try to work side by side with a sport psychologist and I am sure that his contribution will be significant.

If you choose not to work with a psychologist, encourage the players to perform mental preparation, relaxation and the other techniques that appear in this book.

Being only a human being, in most cases you are under the greatest pressure in the whole team!

Stress influences your health and your decision-making.

Functioning under stress for a long time has its influence on health. You should be aware of the fact that heart disease is relatively more common in people with high stress levels.

Leaving health aside, when you are under stress some of the events that happen to players can happen to you and as a result your functioning will be impaired. For example, Phil Jackson (the legendary coach of the Chicago Bulls, the Los Angeles Lakers, and a former player; someone it is difficult to think about as mentally weak), writes in his book that from the beginning of his career as a coach he reach the conclusion that when his heart beat reaches 100 beats per minute, his efficiency as a coach gets hurt. That is the reason that during the game he works on himself in order to lower the level of stress and his heart beat.

If it is true for Phil Jackson, it is certainly true for you too. If you still have doubts about it, check your heart beat several times during a game and you will be surprised from the results (not without a reason you feel exhausted at the end of the game).

In order to be a better coach and a healthier man, it is a must for you too to learn to regulate your stress level.

Remember, all of us are only human beings.

Chapter 9 – Visualization

Visualization is a process that involves imagination. It's the ability to see, hear and feel your actions on a "screen" inside your mind. During this process you perform different actions in order to reach certain goals. It's a thought process of memorizing images and sensations, not words.

Visualization is the exploitation of a wonderful ability that we all carry inside of us, but rarely take advantage of. Visualization is neither a dream nor a fantasy. It's not to say that there is something wrong if an athlete dreams or fantasizes, but it's not what I mean by visualization. The right use of visualization can lead to unimaginable improvement in personal and team performance.

Visualization, like any other skill, should be learned and practiced regularly if you want to have full control over it and receive the most out of it.

The use of visualization for lowering and regulating stress is only one of the possible applications of this process. We can use visualization for:

- Improving personal techniques

- Acquiring new abilities

- Better understanding of the game

- Strengthening our self-confidence and the belief in our abilities

- Improving the team game

- Training for changing game conditions

- Faster recovery after injury

- And more

Every sportsman uses his imagination in one way or another. In this chapter we will learn how to use imagination in the most productive way, we will be acquainted to the basics of visualization and to a number of visualization techniques.

Step 5: Exploit the Power of Visualization

The words visualization and imagination are a bit confusing. Their meaning suggests that we are actually using our visual sense, but it is not true. In visualization we use all of our senses: Vision, Hearing, Smell, Touch and especially the sense of **movement (in order to feel that your leg is moving you don't have to look at it. You feel the movement. When you work with visualization you need to feel the movement you are working with).**

This step will show you how you can combine visualization techniques to be a part of your sport life.

The more senses participate in visualization, the more vivid and successful it will be.

How does visualization regulate and lower stress?

One of the major factors in stress is the lack of certainty – when we don't know what the result will be, how would we perform, etc. Actually, if we knew the score from the beginning, we would not be feeling stress. This is similar to the difference in the tension between watching a game when it's played and watching a game later after the score is already known.

Visualization helps us reduce the uncertainty.

When we speak about increasing our belief in personal and team potential, we use visualization in order to experience the feelings of the different parts of the game. In this way, when we are in the real situation, during the game, our self-confidence and belief in our ability to cope with the situation grow and become stronger.

In this chapter I will try to convince you that not practicing visualization is like not using a specific move or a particular kick in a game to your full ability. We all have the ability to visualize so there is no reason not to practice visualization.

The effect of visualization is always a good feeling of satisfaction and security.

If this is the effect, why not exploit visualization for our good?!

Of course, as of today we don't have a complete scientific explanation of how things we work on in our imagination influence us in the real situations. However, not having a explanation should not prevent us from using visualization.

For example, read the following text and perform the exercise sticking to the instructions:

- Sit comfortably. Close your eyes. And concentrate on your breathing for a minute.
- Clear your mind from the thoughts that occupy it and imagine a picture of a nice yellow lemon. See the yellow lemon in your imagination and try to feel its smell.

- Now, imagine how you bite the lemon.

Feel the taste...

Now very slowly open your eyes.

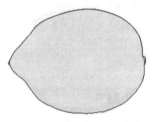

Did you succeed in seeing the lemon?

What did you feel when you bit it?

Most of us feel the bitter taste

of the lemon, did you feel it too?

Did the expression on your face express

that you ate something bitter?

If you didn't feel a thing, don't be discouraged, with time and exercise, your ability to exploit imagination will grow and develop.

How it is possible that the lemon we saw only in our vision made us taste its bitterness?

To feel the taste, wasn't it necessary to have the food touch the taste buds on our tongue?

As I said, we do not have an explanation for this, but visualization has its influence on reality. This is the reason for the importance of working with visualization in soccer.

What you practice in your imagination will directly influence your performance.

The principles of visualization – rules for correct practice.

1. You are the producer of the movie you choose to work on. Pick up any situation of the game you are interested in.

2. Short visualization (up to a minute) can be done on the field without relaxation.

3. Long visualization (up to 5 minutes) is performed in a state of relaxation. In means that you need to start with a full or shortened relaxation exercise and performance visualization after it.

4. Visualization is done with eyes closed. Desirably when seated or lying.

5. Don't perform visualization continuously for more than 3 to 5 minutes. After visualizing revert to relaxation. And finish with visualization for a couple of minutes.

6. Visualization is done always in the present. In other words, you say to yourself "I am now in the game", "It happen right now" etc.

7. In visualization we practice specific actions and just a few pictures. We don't deal with a long movie (this means that we can visualize our heading towards the goalkeeper, and we can work on an attack with no more than 10 passes). That is why you have to

choose a specific goal for each visualization you perform.

8. The imagination of your actions should be done in real speed.(not slow motion).

9. Performing visualization should take into account your actual talents and abilities. Don't imagine that you run as fast as the world champion 100-meter sprinter and don't see yourself jump for a ball as the high jump world champion. Performing visualization should be fitted to your best performance, with a small add-on.

10. Imagine yourself always succeeding when visualizing.

11. Be sure that you perform your actions correctly in visualization. If you work in imagination with the wrong technique, you can achieve the opposite result – strengthening the wrong technique.

12. The more senses you use in visualization, the more effective it will be. It is especially important to incorporate the sense of movement. When you imagine a head er, feel the movements you do (hopping, body prepa ration and performing the skill), see the picture and hear the noise of the heading. The more "live" your visualization is, the more efficient it will be!

13. You can perform visualization while you see yourself from the side (run with the ball like we see on TV) or you can see the situation as if through your own eyes during the game (when you don't see yourself, but the field, the other players etc.). Both ways are good, but for most people it is easier to perform visualiza-

tion from outside. In any case, choose the way that you feel comfortable with and allow yourself to go from one way to the other.

Visualization from outside
You see yourself like on TV, with the camera following you.

Visualization from inside
You see the ball, the goal, the camera is situated on your head.

13. **While visualizing you are alert like in the real situation. When you revert to relaxation, you will relax.**
15. **Visualization does not offer a substitute for training and practice on the field. It is intended to improve, to strengthen and to focus you.**

The major visualization you will perform is the imagination of different game situations. Regular practice in visualization will lead to a situation in which the things you practice in your mind will happen in reality, your self-confidence and belief in success will be much stronger.

Visualization makes it possible to deal with familiar situations that you have already encountered in the past and you feel you have the right solution for them.

Following are some examples of possible game situations. These are only examples. As I said, you are the producer of your visualization. It is up to you to choose the game situations according to your performance on the field and according to the skills you want to improve. This is a model of visualization work for 12 minutes.

Read the exercise to its end before you try to perform it.

Example for work with visualization

1. Sit down or lie comfortably, close your eyes and concentrate on your breathing.
2. Go with your thoughts through your whole body from the head to the feet and check that nothing is tense or tight.
3. Relax your body. Concentrate on your breath and take 4 deep breaths. Enter the air very slowly through your nose and feel your chest rise. Continue breathing in air until you feel that your belly rises as well.
4. Stop for a few seconds and exhale the air very slowly and continuously.
5. Perform 3 additional deep breaths.
6. Concentrate now on your regular breathing and start counting your breaths from now on. Every time you breathe in, count in your mind, the first time 1, the second 2 and so on, till you reach 10. Then start counting again from the beginning. Perform this 3 times (3 times 10).
7. Concentrate on your breathing. Stop counting your breaths and start working with your imagination: It happens exactly right now. You see yourself enter the field. You feel the movement and hear the voices. You are concentrated on yourself and full of belief in your ability. You had good games in the past and this is going to be a good game too. Tell yourself a

couple of times: I believe in my abilities, I will give a good game.

See yourself in the game, It happens to you right now. See yourself in the opponent's part of the field and see yourself go for the ball. Feel the movements you perform. You rise for a high ball, prepare your body and head for a goal. Feel the movement, hear the contact with the ball and listen to the roar of the crowd. Return to the final touch a couple of times, from different places on the field and with balls of different heights...

8. Now, allow the image to disappear and put your thoughts aside.

9. Concentrate on your regular breathing and start counting your breaths. Count twice to 10 and concentrate again on your breathing.

You are now in the game, it happens to you exactly right now. You are attacking the opponent. See yourself moving, receive the ball, make a move and kick for a goal. Feel the move ment. Feel the movement of your leg in the kick, hear the bump of the kick and listen to the roar of the crowd. Return over it a few times from different places on the field, look at different kinds of movement you use, variety of kicks and all that is related...

You are playing right now, it happens to you in this moment. Look at the player and at the color of his clothes. See your-self completely calm, perform a feint and pass the ball pre cisely. It happens in this very moment, feel the movement. Go over the situation a couple of times, from different places on the field, in different game positions...

10. Now, let the images disappear and allow your thoughts to be free. Concentrate on your regular breathing and start counting your breaths. Count twice till 10 and concentrate on your breath.

    You are on the field now, it happens to you in this very moment. Watch yourself perform defensive actions. Look at your opponent trying to pass you. Watch yourself do the right move, save the ball and pass it over. Look at you again and again. Right now, an opposing player is trying to pass around you, but you are concentrated on the ball and his attempt to avoid you is futile. You go for the ball and save it. You are aggressive and determined. You save the ball and pass it precisely. Watch yourself again and again, in different places on the field…

11. Now, let the images disappear slowly and concentrate on your breathing. Let the tension leave you. Concentrate on your breathing and count 10 breaths. Stop counting and breathe one slow deep breath. While you breathe in an image of one of your good moves from a previous game enters your imagination. A good move - one that filled you with a pleasant feeling, confidence and belief in your abilities. Keep the image in your mind and while breathing experience the feeling you felt when you made the move…

12. Let the image disappear and concentrate on your breathing… Tell yourself a couple of times: "I'm positive about my abilities, I will have a good game". Now, with every breath you take, your self-confidence strengthens and grows. And together with it grows your belief in personal ability. It is clear to you that your next game will be a great game. Bring up to

imagination your stress meter and look what it shows. Concentrate on it and bring it to the measure fitting your maximum performance. If you are still far away from the right measure, continue with the relaxation exercise until you reach the right value...

13. Now, concentrate on your breathing and very slowly open your eyes.

Practice the visualization exercise right now following the instructions and its principles. Do it according to your abilities. It need not follow the instructions exactly, but keep the following rules:

- Work in the present
- Use as many senses as possible
- Train on short situations
- Revert to relaxation for several minutes
- Perform with the right intensity and speed
- Succeed in every action
- Adjust the game situations you train on to your position in the game

Perform this now and when you finish return to reading.

How do you feel?

In most cases, even from the first time and without following these principles exactly, you experience a pleasant feeling, the self-confidence grows and with it personal ability becomes stronger. If the game was beginning right now, for sure you would have played a good game. A good and pleasant feeling.

With results like these, why don't you adopt the method and train regularly in visualization?

The more you train you will perform visualization better and your improved performance on the field will be the best proof that visualization works and you become a better player.
In chapter 25 you will find examples of visualization exercises for players in different game positions.

An additional way to work with visualization is teamwork.
In a situation that players want to work with visualization together, it is possible that one of them will give the instructions and the rest will practice.
It is recommended to work on elements of the game connected to group performance, even when you train alone. In such situations you practice with visualization on short episodes of the game in which you don't see yourself alone, but also the position and movement of the rest of the players. You see their movement relative to your position and movements. In such a moment you can work on movement without the ball, in order to receive a good pass and later while running with the ball to pass it exactly, knowing precisely where all the players are situated, even if you cannot see them. **In a similar way you can work on your defense together with the whole team.**
Work with visualization on the performance of your team. The position of the players in changing game conditions and the position of the opponents will improve your understanding of the

game, lower your reaction time and make it possible
to you to pass the ball precisely.

Additional types of visualization:

1. Visualization of learning and practicing a new skill – **you saw a Nigerian player jump with the ball and you want to try it too. Work on the exercise with visualization following the rules above. Be strict on using your sense of movement. Perform the action in imagination several times and of course, practice it on the field as well.**

2. Visualization of an ideal model – **if we continue with the previous example, see in visualization again and again the player perform the movement and from time to time see yourself perform it.**

3. Visualization of a perfect performance – **choose an image of a perfect performance of yours (a perfect header, an exact kick, a flawless move, a save etc.). We speak about performance after which you felt great happiness, satisfaction and belief in your ability. In short a great feeling. Choose an image or a couple of images and visualize them every time your confidence is low and always in the minutes before the beginning of the game. When you perform the visualization use all your senses (listen to the announcer, to the audience and feel your movements, see the whole picture…). Feel exactly like you felt when you did the action in reality.**

4. Visualization before performance - **in situations in which this is possible, especially in static situations, perform short visualization before the real performance and then do this in reality. It is possible to do so before a penalty**

kick, a side kick, a throw in, etc. **Visualization is done just before the performance. This way it will be similar to performance in imagery (decide exactly where you want the ball to go, kick in visualization feeling the movement, see the ball go exactly where you planned it to go).** The use of such a technique will improve your performance drastically. **So why don't you try it? For example, in kick training** choose where you want the ball to go. **If you kick towards the goal, choose to kick in the upper right corner. Kick 10 times in the regular way and remember how many times you succeeded... now do exactly the same kick only before each kick imagine it.** See yourself kick exactly in the desired spot, feel the

movement you do and then kick the ball. **Count the times you succeeded from 10 kicks. I promise you improved performance (preciseness, power, etc.) already from the first try.**

5. Visualization as if... - **this is a different kind of visualization in the sense that you don't close your eyes, but perform it in the game. If you want to be more aggressive while already in the game, imagine yourself** like a tiger jumping on his prey. **If you want to be more plastic, see yourself** like a rubber band. **If you feel tired, imagine you are** an animal defending his cubs. **If you need a faster start, imagine you are** a rushing cheetah. **It is recommended to adopt a picture of something that is typical for you. Choose the right image for you and for the goal you want to achieve.** When the game is difficult and you do not succeed, return to the image you chose and imagine yourself in it, even during the game.

6. Reversed visualization – **sometimes it is important to go back in imagination over an action you already per-formed in order to correct a mistake. This is done in order to see the fault and immediately correct it by visu-alizing the performance the way you wanted to perform it. This way raises the chance that our achievements will be better in the following occasions.**

7. Visualizing long game episodes – **I said earlier that it is advisable to work on single images and short game situ-ations and usually this is the right practice, except these cases in which we want to analyze the game and to learn from our mistakes. It can be done watching the game on video or with the help of our imagination. We can recon-struct parts of the game and not only the images but also our feelings and thoughts at the time. It is important to remember what was our decision and then try to see in imagination what was the mistake, in order to be able to fix it in the future.**

8.<u>**Visualizing the safe place**</u> – **this is one of** the most important types of visualization and it is necessary for every athlete and every man. **Phil Jackson the ex-coach of the "Chicago Bulls" used to perform it regularly with his players (yes with Rodman, Pippen and Jordan). In his book he writes that in time outs during the game, when he feels that the confidence and concentration of his players has lowered, he sits them on the bench and requires them to visualize the safe place. If it is good for them, almost perfect players, then for sure it is good for us too.**

In this visualization you choose yourself a personal safe place. **It can be a real or imagined place. It can be a pic-ture of your mother**  **hugging you or breast feeding you, a pic-ture of a girl friend or a woman hugging you, or it can be your favorite room in the house, a beach, an island or any other place. What is impor-tant is to choose a place where you felt safe/ protected/ full of self-confidence – in short a perfect feeling. Every time it is difficult or you feel everything goes against you, take yourself with the help of imagination for a couple of seconds to this place. Take yourself to the safe place together with the perfect feeling that this place makes you feel and in this way you will come back from there to the game full of belief in your ability and with maximum motivation. Train this visualization several times and dis-cover how powerful and useful it is.**

9. Treating an injury with visualization – **in the same way we do not understand how from an imagined picture of a lemon we can taste its bitterness, we cannot explain how imagination influences the treatment of the body. What is important for us is the fact that imagination can influence and make faster the recovery from injury. With this kind of visualization I will deal later in the book in the chapter dealing with injuries and their treatment (Chapter 20).**

Since the profit we can gain from the use of visualization is huge and its practice is pleasant, we don't have any reason not to practice it. In this chapter I mentioned the coach of the "Chicago Bulls" who used visualization with his team.

Today this is a common practice in the top-level teams in every sport. Sometimes we can see athletes performing visualization during   contests. This kind of visualization is especially distinct for the jump athletes: high-jump, long jump and pole-vault. It is possible to see them performing visualization moments before running for the jump. However, as I said, not only athletes of this branch of athletics do so. The best athletes in the world from all kinds of sports use visualization as an indivisible part of their training program.

Visualization can be done in any situation, you don't need a trainer or a psychologist, nor any equipment or special conditions. Everything you need is always with you – every thing is inside your mind. All you need is the desire to use this technique and to practice and practice it.

Summary

In the beginning of the book I promised you that you could improve your ability if you adopt
only a part of what I am offering you.
Visualization is an important part of this:
Constant use of visualization guarantees an improvement in your ability.

- Visualization is the most important
and efficient mental technique.
- Adopt working with visualization –
and improved ability is guaranteed.
- Visualization can be done at any place
in every situation.

- Working with visualization is pleasant.
- Visualization should be done according the rules
for achieving maximum efficiency.
- It is important to use as many senses
as possible in visualization.
- It is important to practice it again and again.
The practice improves your ability to visualize and
this perfects the results too. Thanks to that the
improvement in your ability will grow.

Visualization Of Success Shortens The Way To Success

The Coach Box

Visualization is not intended only for the players. Visualization is an instrument for you and for any other person. As a coach you have to encourage your players to work with visualization and as for yourself the use of visualization can calm you and help you function much better. The use of visualization of the safe place will help you cope better with stress and for sure will contribute to your decision taking abilities.

Exactly as players work with visualization over difficult game situations, you too can work with visualization over different game situations from your point of view. You should emphasize analysis of the game and decision making but also control over your emotions, concentration and more.

Work with visualization will make it possible for you:
To regulate your stress.

To control your emotions during the game.

To improve your concentration.

To improve your decision taking abilities.

In short, not only will visualization make you a better man,
it will turn you into a better coach.

Chapter 10 – Control Your Thoughts

In chapter 7 we saw that the major stress factor for a soccer player is the player himself. A player has enough good reasons to feel stress: the coach, the press, the fans, the game itself, his teammates, the opposing players, the fear of injury and many more. All these are good reasons to be stressed, but it is a fact that not all players feel the same level of stress.

As a matter of fact:

The meaning you give to what happens around you and in your mind is the reason for the stress you feel.

We speak about your thoughts and
about the things you say to yourself.
These factors can advance you or destroy you as a player!

When stress exists we have trouble coping with it. We can try to prevent stress or regulate it to the needed level using control over our thoughts. In this chapter we will try to learn to use our thoughts and talking to ourselves as instruments for stress regulation and mental preparation for the game.

Step 6: Face Your Thoughts And Control Them

Stress is a sign for a challenge

Learn to give a different definition to the situation!
When your stress level crosses the line of maximum performance, you can try to disregard the feeling of stress, but as we saw, this denial won't solve a thing.

Another possible way is to let the stress overwhelm you because you are tense. It really sounds strange, but it happens to a lot of players. After the player reaches the conclusion that stress hinders him from showing his maximum performance, immediately thoughts like "I'm too stressed", "I cannot play well in this game", "The game is lost for me", "We are going to lose" and so on arise. Of course, these thoughts only increase and reinforce the stress.

The correct way to deal with this situation is first to admit the existence of stress and to try to regulate it to the desired level with the help of relaxation and visualization. Additionally, it is possible and necessary to give a different explanation to stress.

Our thoughts lead our body to recognize the situation as stressful and to respond to it accordingly.

If you teach yourself to give different explanations to the situation, your reaction will change as well!

In the usual situation you put yourself in a "magic circle":

Situation (an important game)

Mistake

Defining
the situation
(can't lose)

Stress

The **definition** you give to the **situation** (the game, the score, what the coach said etc) **causes** you to feel **stress**. The feeling of tension brings with it the **stress reaction** of the body that prevents you from playing well and leads you to make **mistakes**. That in the light of your definition of the situation, ("Can't lose this game") will strengthen the feeling of stress and so on. **In other words you are in a "magic circle" that cannot be broken**.

Your performance in the game will eventually lead the coach to take you out of the game!

The only way to keep from entering this "magic circle" is to cut it right from its beginning. You can do this if you change the situation definition or the explanation you give to it.

Instead of looking at the situation as stressful, outline it as an opportunity to prove your ability.

Only in this way can you break the circle. However, it is not so simple. During the years your mind has become used to explaining situations as stressful and because of that the first automatic explanation that enters your mind is the interpretation of stress. In order to change this habit and bring a different definition, **you should be aware** of what is happening and search consciously for an **alternative thought**.

If you recognize and change the automatic meaning for your situation every time, with time you will succeed in changing for good. One of the ways to change your situation definition is to use stress as an indicator that when you feel your stress level is high, then the game is especially important for you.

When I'm under stress, this is a sign for me that this game is going to be a challenge for me. And this is my chance now to demonstrate my ability.

It is enough to say "This game is a challenge for me. I'm capable of taking the challenge. This will be a good game for me." in order to change the feeling of stress into a feeling of challenge. In such a way, every time the level of stress rises repeat to yourself several times this sentence with full belief in your ability and completely sure in your success. If you do so, you will see how it will influence your game performance immediately.

<u>Stress = Chance = Challenge</u>

Situation (an important game)

Low Stress   **Stress**

Defining the situation <u>challenge</u>

It is possible to turn the feeling of stress into a piston that pushes you forward, instead of a press that crushes you deep into the ground.

As the source of the problem lies in you, so does its solution – everything depends on the explanation you give to your feelings.

If you follow this technique, the challenge and not the stress will turn out to be the essential part of your sporting life. Your automatic reaction to stress will be the filling of challenge!

Thought and positive self-talk

Every player has thoughts about what is going to be in the coming game and every player expresses his thoughts with words. In other words, every player talks to himself.

Without a reason, our first automatic reaction in a situation is to give it a negative explanation. We bring up negative thoughts and utter to ourselves negative sentences. For example, when somebody close to you is late for a meeting with you (except a few players who are always late and this example is not intended about them) the first thought that enters your mind is that something bad might have happened to him. "Maybe he had an accident." "He probably got hurt" and so on. The more time passes, our thoughts become worse and worse and the feeling of stress grows.

Reason says that in fact we don't have any reason to think negatively.
In most cases the chances that something good happened are no different than the chances that something bad happened.

In other words, a woman whose husband is very late starts to worry and immediately is flooded with thoughts that something bad has happened or that perhaps he is with someone else. For some reason, the thought that "Maybe he went to buy me a nice present" or any other positive thought does not enter her mind.

**In sport, negative thinking and pessimistic self-talk
increase the players feeling of stress.
They harm his concentration, self-confidence and
weaken his belief in personal ability.**

That's why it is important to recognize the negative thoughts and sayings and to try to change them. You can do this if you adopt strategies for dealing with these thoughts and sayings. These strategies will cause your negative thoughts and ideas to disappear and positive thoughts and sayings will take their place. If your thoughts before the game are: "I'm not capable", "We are going to lose", "We don't have a chance against a team like this", "I can't guard this player, because he is fast/strong/big", "I never succeed against this team", "On this field I don't play well", "I cannot score a goal with this goal keeper" and more, you have already hurt your chances in advance to show your maximum ability. These thoughts lead you to unnecessary stress, impair your concentration and undermine your self-confidence and the belief in your ability.

**When you start the game with negative thoughts,
even before entering the field you "score a self-goal"
because these thoughts fulfill themselves.**

**These negative thoughts drag you into a "magic circle"
and it is very difficult to get out of it.**

Thought ("I'm not capable")

Stress   **Mistake**

Self-fulfilling Thought

If you thought while talking to yourself that against that team you never succeed and after a couple of minutes you made a mistake in the game, you received proof that you were right and against this team you can't win. Now, you have one more reason to think this way and your stress will grow. As a result your concentration will be hurt and you will make the same mistake again, one more example that you were right... In other words, it is clear that with such thoughts you can't have a good game.

If you really didn't have a good game and your team lost then after the game you have more good evidence for what you thought.

When you prepare for the following game the negative thoughts enter your mind again and it will be extremely difficult to stop them. The right way to treat them is to be conscious about these thoughts, **to express them and change them immediately**. To turn them right away into positive thoughts and optimistic self-talk.

> **You can't allow the negative thoughts to gain control over your thinking.**

It may sound simple, but because of our tendency to bring automatically negative thoughts to our mind and because of our experience and habits we have developed through the years, it is very difficult to change this type of thinking. **It is hard but it is possible.**

Like every change and learning of a new technique there is a need for a lot of practice and training to control our thoughts. In this way we can replace every negative thought with a positive one. To do this you need to know two basic rules:

Rule One – Don't accept negative thoughts or pessimistic self-talk. You must change them into positive thoughts and self-talk. Be careful that the **last word or thought is always positive**.

Rule Two – Concentrate only on the present, not on the past and not in the future (for example, previous bad games on this field or against this team or bad expectations like "What if we lose?" etc.).

This rule is true also about mistakes you make during the game. You have to continue and concentrate only on the present and immediately forget any wrong move you've done.

Step 7 Change your negative thoughts into positive

The way to achieve control over your thoughts is through work, practice and training. Negative thoughts and self-talk enter your mind during practice too and without any connection to sport. Start paying attention to what you think and tell yourself and use every opportunity to replace the negative thoughts with positive. Be careful, keep your thoughts in the present and learn to say "Stop!" to yourself.

 Every time a negative thought enters your mind you should tell yourself **"Stop!"** and replace it with a positive thought. Every time you think about the past or the future you should say **"Stop!"** and take yourself back to the present and what is happening now. **If you persist and train you will gradually attain control over your thoughts and will reach a state in which you won't have to change your thoughts and inner talk, because they always will be positive and you won't need to use the word "Stop!".**

These are a few examples of negative thoughts/sayings before a game and their opposite positives:

<u>Negative thoughts/sayings:</u>

We are never lucky against this team.

We lost against them last year.

The pressure is too high. I can't make it.

I never succeed on this field.

We always give up goals in the last minutes.

I can't play well in rain.

<u>Positive thoughts/sayings</u>

I believe in my ability in every game.

Every game starts 0 : 0 and what will be will be.

Stress is a challenge for me. I can regulate it.

I can guard any player.

I believe in my ability on every field.

We will play concentrated and confident till the end whistle.

I believe in my ability in any situation.

A good way to cope with negative thoughts is to prepare in advance a list of positive sayings and to repeat them a couple of times a day, at the end of relaxation exercise and when negative thoughts enter your mind. The sayings should be short, positive, about you and the present. Here are some examples:

- I believe in my ability in every situation
- I believe in the ability of the team
- I'm aggressive and determined in
  defense and attack.
- I see the whole field.
- Nobody can beat me.
- I get help from the other players.

- I do my personal and team duties.
- I play and don't give up till the whistle.

Repeat again and again sayings of this type – you are welcome to compose your own sayings – and they will remain constant in your mind and will have a positive influence on you.

Summary

- What you think will decide if you win or lose.
- Learn to explain every stressful situation as **a challenge**.
- Believe in your ability and it won't be difficult to face the challenge.
- With the right work on your thoughts you will have **more challenges** and less stress.
- Always think **positive**.
- Think only about the **present**.
- Replace every negative thought with a **positive**.
- Learn to say **"Stop!"** to yourself.
- It is necessary to practice the **control over your thought**s at every chance.

The Coach Box

A lot of times what a player thinks about himself is influenced by what you transmit to him. If what he receives from you (even if you do not intend it) is the feeling or understanding that he is a failure, that he is not a good player or that it is not worth investing in him, he might think this way about himself as well.

It is your right and duty to take a player from the team line-up when he is not fit or does not follow your instructions, etc. but it is forbidden to turn him into a failure.

It is important that the player understands that there is a direct connection between his game and your decision and there is not any other reason. Not less important, the player should understand that his return to the line-up depends on his ability and the work he will do.

I mentioned earlier that it is very important for a player to concentrate on the present, on what is happening now on the field and not on what already happened. Some coaches make it difficult for the players to concentrate on the present when during the game they continue yelling at them about mistakes ...and continue yelling and yelling. The only thing you can achieve in this way is to hurt the concentration of the players and increase the chances for mistakes.

If a player made a mistake and it is important to you to correct it during the game (and the emphasis is during the game and not in the break or the next day in the morning) – do this in a way that will help him continue the game. A good approach to do so is the following:

- Call the player to come to you (when it is possible)
- Tell him a positive sentence ("You're working hard")
- Correct his mistake ("Next time save some energy and
  kick the ball out...")
- Finish with a positive sentence ("Come on, I believe
  in you!")

Behaviors such as yelling in every direction or running wildly on the lines won't be effective and will only disturb the players.

If you adopt this attitude, you will achieve results and your players will respect you more.

Chapter 11 – Plan and Analyze

We have seen that one of the major reasons for stress in soccer is the uncertainty. One way to deal with it is visualization. Together with visualization we should exploit our ability to think and analyze in order to prepare for the game and lower the uncertainty.

Step 8 : Use your mind/your head in preparation for the game and during the game

In order to complete this task you need the following information:
- Know the opponent you are playing against and especially his style of play and the players with whom you will come in close contact.
- Recognize the role the coach has given you for the coming game and how he wants you to perform it

The knowledge about your opponent you can receive from the coach or alone watching previous games of the opposing team or from personal experience from previous games. The coach will explain your role in the game to you. In order to prepare better for the game it is advisable to know your role, including the special emphasis for the coming game, as early as possible. In case the coach does not inform the players who is in the line-up you can speak with him and ask him a question of the kind: "If I play a right defender in the coming game, what would you expect from me?" etc.

After you have the information about your opponent and your playing position, try to think how you can perform your duties in a better way. Check with yourself what worked in the previous games and what didn't work. Try to think which problems might occur to you during the game and what could be their possible solutions. Prepare for yourself solutions for the different game situations and be ready for surprises that the opponent can prepare.

Your goal is not to be surprised in the game.
A surprised player is a player in trouble!

If you were sure that the defender on your side does not usually attack and you did not prepare for such a situation, but to your surprise the defender attacks time after time – you are in trouble. It is very difficult to change things already in the game. That's why it is preferable to prepare in advance for all the possibilities and not to be surprised on the field.

It is true that a significant part of the preparation lies on your coach and should be done by him. However, at the end, you will be on the field against the opponent and not the coach. For this reason the responsibility for your preparation should fall entirely on you.

The coach can help you, but he cannot prepare for you.

It is important to understand that even if you play a steady role in the team and in every game you play in the same position (defender, mid-fielder, forward), after all every game is a **new game**. And in every game the way you carry out your duty changes according to the opponent. Of course the difference can be small or big, according to your coach's decision, and you have to **be ready** for this.

After you have collected the information (talked to the coach, watched the previous games on video, etc.), analyze it and think about the way you will perform your duty in the best possible way.

Use the days before the game for visualizing yourself performing your role, including possible surprises.

The combination of thought work and visualization training will prepare you in the best way for the game. It will lower the feeling of stress and will significantly increase the belief in your ability to play your part of the game in the best possible way.

During the game he should find the time to think and ask

Thinking and analyzing do not end with the beginning of the game.
A player who wants to be mentally strong and wants to improve his ability on the field must bring his mind/head with him to the field.

"Who is doing what?". He should check if he performs his duty as the coach expects (he should make his own conclusions without waiting for the shout of the coach). He thinks what the opponent does, what succeeds and what doesn't.

Thinking and analyzing during the game will prevent you from getting into trouble, will lower the stress and will make it possible to be a better player.

Summary

- Planning and analyzing are an important
part of your mental preparation.
- You are responsible for your preparation
before each game.
- You should prepare for playing your part
before each game.
- A good player thinks before and during the game.
- Learn to ask yourself during the game:
"Who did what and why?".

The Coach Box

Your job as a trainer is to help the players prepare mentally for the game. Give your players the information they need, so that they can prepare for the game as early as possible.

It is your duty to require from the players **to think** before and during the game.

Don't keep your tactical lesson for the last minute. In order that your players can be prepared, they need to practice the tactics in their training and with visualization. If your habit is to announce the line-up in the last moment you make it difficult for the players to prepare. In such a situation you can give the information to the team without announcing the opening line-up. A sentence like: "I expect from the left defender…" etc

Chapter 12 – Regulating the Pressure

Step 9: Be aware of your personal stress level and regulate it to best fit your abilities

Regulating stress in the changing room, before the game.

With the right practice during the week (in the last chapter I offer a weekly program for mental preparation), the goal is to be ready for a game from all aspects and of course mentally, including your stress level regulated to your desired level. In this way, you would not have any particular trouble before a game.

Regardless of this, during your preparation for the game in the changing room you need to continue to work on your mental preparation with the help of relaxation and visualization. **Check again your stress-meter**.

It is recommended to invest the last 5 – 10 minutes, after you have finished changing and have done the stretches and the warm up, in an attempt to regulate your tension and to bring it to the most suitable level for your performance.

When you are in the dressing room and there are only a couple of minutes before the game your stress is at its highest. In order to control it, you must be well trained. **Don't expect to regulate stress if you don't train all week, all season**. Don't try to use the methods I offer you for the first time 10 minutes before you enter an important game. The chance that you will succeed is less than meager.

> **In mental training as in fitness training
> there are no shortcuts or magic remedies.**

Facing stress and pressure on the field.

Sometimes, even after the best preparation the stress level you take with you to the field will prevent you from showing your maximum ability.

At other times, stress can rise during the game, because of the score, the course of the game or the thoughts that rise in you.

The first step is **to recognize** that your stress level is too high and the second is an attempt to regulate it, through the game.

The Self – Check

After you have worked out your stress level to suit your maximum performance in the dressing room, check yourself in order to confirm that you have reached the desired level. If you conclude that your stress is higher than before your good games this means that your stress level is too high. If the measure is lower it is a sign that your stress level is too low and you have to raise it up. If the measures are the same you have succeeded in regulating stress to the desired level and you are ready for the game (during the game you must be conscious about the signs of stress and its level, because as I said, stress can change during the game).

The first stage in the attempt to regulate stress is during the warm up you do on the field.

Lowering Stress

- Concentrate in the warm up. **The more stressed you feel- work harder in the warm up**. During the warm up concentrate on your body feelings. Concentrate on the sensation of your legs, stomach and hands and try to block any other thoughts about the game and its result.

- Start talking to yourself about positive things. Tell yourself things like: "I believe in my abilities", "The stress I feel will only make me play better", "My self-confidence is high, this will be a good game for me" etc. Always say this in a **positive way** and always only in **the present**.
- While you are stretching, take deep breaths and feel how your body becomes more and more fit for the game and how your stress decreases to a level that will allow you to show maximum performance.
- While lying down close your eyes and bring to your imagination an image of one of your successful actions from a previous game. Feel the good feeling that you felt when you succeeded and with the image in your mind take a deep breath and say "Now, I feel exactly like I felt in the action in my mind".
- Open your eyes. Every time you breathe in the belief in your ability will grow and breathing out you will feel how stress is released and leaves you.
- Check the stress meter. Did the stress level reach the level best suited to your ability? If not repeat the exercise.
- Moments before the whistle, visualize again one of your good actions.

Increasing Stress

When your stress level is lower than necessary for maximum performance try to think what are the reasons for this:

- **Are you indifferent because you are sure you will lose today?**
- **Are you sure your team will win and you underestimate the opposing team?**
- **Are you angry at the coach/the other players and you don't care what will happen in the game?**

Try to find the reason and accordingly try to cancel it.

- Exactly like in the case of high stress start with a very intensive warm up. This way while your body gets hotter your mind too heats up and the stress level rises.

- During the warmup start talking to yourself positively, concentrating only on the present and on your will to show your maximum ability. Without any connection to the reason your stress level is low, the reason is always based on the past (for example, the opponent is strong or weak), tell yourself that the past is in the past. In this game everything is possible. Forget the past and concentrate on the present.

- While stretching tell yourself that you are tightening your muscles including the muscle in your head. You prepare it now for the game and you fit it to the exact stress level for your maximum performance.

- Take deep breaths and with each breath feel how your mind and body become more and more focused for the game.

- Check your stress meter. Did the stress reach the suitable level for your performance? If not repeat the exercise.

- Seconds before the whistle visualize a positive move.

Coping with stress during the game

During the game you usually are under higher and not lower stress. A too-high stress level in the beginning of the game or at any point during the game will hurt your concentration, prevent you from achieving your maximum ability and cause you to make mistakes.

It is important to remember the signs of stress and how they appear in players during the game:
- Exaggerated Aggressiveness
- Low reaction threshold (cursing, shouting, etc.)
- Gets rid of every ball
- Does not advance to receive the ball
- Feeling of heavy legs
- Lack of air
- Different mistakes

If you recognize the stress signs, you should try to **perform simple actions** in the first minutes of the game instead of trying complex moves. A simple and exact pass is preferable to a failed attempt to pass the ball 30 meters between two defenders. It is better to kick the ball out than to try a difficult move that will not work.

Since you are not fully concentrated, the more complicated actions you take lower the chance for success, because these actions require a high level of concentration.

After a few minutes and several successful actions, the level of stress will drop and you will be able to play your usual game. Because of this, until the stress drops down take advantage of every possible moment (for example, when the ball is far away from you, ball from the side, treating a player etc.) to take **deep breaths**.

In this stage, when the stress is high and your concentration is not at its best force yourself to be concentrated on the ball or a player – actions that in the usual situation you perform without any effort and automatically. Force yourself to be concentrated and tell yourself "Concentrate on the Ball", when you go for the ball or when you are going for a header, a shot, etc.

Slowly and continuously the pressure will drop down and you will start playing your regular game. During the game be attentive about what is happening to you. Be careful that pressure will not drop too much. In cases like this, stress lowers, concentration suffers and your situation can turn from advantage into a drawback.

Don't let pressure drop too much! Be aware of your stress level and keep it throughout the game close to the level that best fits your maximum ability.

Summary

- With the right practice during the week you will prevent problems on game day
- Perform visualization and relaxation in the dressing room.
- Always check your stress level and strictly regulate it to the level fitting your maximum performance.
- The moment you enter the field check your stress level again.

- Use the warm up for regulating stress.

**- During the game be aware of your stress level
and regulate it accordingly.**

- Be careful not to let pressure drop too much

The Coach Box

The team preparation for the game is your responsibility but it is your duty to place a bit of responsibility on each player as well. You should help each player in his preparation. You can do this by helping him with **information about the opposing team, especially about the players that he will have contact with and of course explaining to him his duty in the game and placing clear goals for the coming game**.

One of the ways to cope with the stress and pressure in the game is the **proper preparation during the training**. The army saying "Difficult in the training, easy in the fight" is true about sport as well.

If the training is close or exceeds in its difficulty and intensity what is expected from the game it will be easier in the game.

Practice games that the team plays with itself should be as close as possible to the real game from all points of view: motivation, aggressiveness, etc.

I was surprised to see that players tend to play in practice games without protective pads. **Their excuse was that it is uncomfortable to play with the pads, however this is exactly the reason they should practice with them.**

A game without protective pads lowers in advance the intensity of the game because of the concern about injuries and does not prepare the players for the real game.

In most of the training games and in most teams the coach plays the starting eleven against the bench. Such an exercise has a lot of importance – the players who play together in the game should play together in practice too. However, training has other goals besides the team practice.

Generally, it is true to say that the level of the bench players will be lower than the level of the players of the opposing team and the practice game won't be close to the coming game. In order to prepare the team better it is possible to change the line-up in different parts of the training, for example to exchange the forwards of the two teams. In this way, the defenders and forwards of the opening team will have a better practice. You can also place special restrictions on the starting eleven. For example, to let them play with less players or to play against more players.

Usually you can make a better use of the second team. You can instruct its players to play in the way the upcoming opponent is expected to play and to insist on an intensive and aggressive game.

Some of the players from the second team will be substitutes in the coming game and there is a reasonable chance they will be joined during the game. That is why you are obliged to let them practice with the starting line-up.

Efficient use of your second team will not only help in the team preparation, but will also contribute to the team consolidation, heightening the motivation of all the players and improving the feelings inside the team.

The following chapter deals with the topic of "team".

Chapter 13 –
You Need A "TEAM" for a Team game

Soccer is a team game and there should be a team to play soccer.

What is a team?

A team is first of all a group of players.

Is every group of players a team?

No, absolutely not! In order that a group of players should become a team there are 3 conditions to be fulfilled:

1. **They should have a common goal.**
2. **In order to achieve the goal the players should depend on each other.**
3. **There should be interrelationships between the players. The action of one of them must influence the others.**

The understanding of **all the partners** to the team – and I mean **all the partners** and not only all the players (including all the coaches, the management, the owners, the doctor, the psychologist etc.) of these principles is essential for the success of the team.

Of special importance is the understanding of the principle of interrelationship and dependency between the members of the team who are striving for a goal.

A good team is a team in which the team ability is bigger than the sum of the personal ability of the players. In other words, the whole is bigger than the sum of its parts. In practical terms this means that if we give to each player in the team a score about his best performance and we add all of the scores together (let's say marks from 1 to 10 for each player, so that we can have a maximum of 110 points) we will get a score about the team ability between 11 and 110. You can not deny that **in a good team the team ability score will be higher than the sum of the single players' scores and in a bad team the team score will be lower than the sum of the single players.**

When speaking about professional soccer, turning a group of players into a team is the main task of the coach, but **there is also importance in every single player's contribution for the building of the team.**

The word building is not good enough, because it implies a process with a beginning and end. And it is not this way with a team.

When we speak about a **team this is a process that continues all the time.** It is true that before the beginning of the season in practice and training camps the emphasis on developing the team will be stronger, but this must be a continuous process.

It is much easier to destroy a team than to build one.

The destruction of a team can happen at any moment in the season because of the action of players, the management or the coaches.

How can it be that an excellent bunch of players will not make a good team?

It's a fact! There are plenty of examples of teams that invested huge amounts of money in attracting good players and did not succeed in building a good team.

If we build a team from the world's best players, will it be the best team in the world?

Not necessarily. It will be a good team if enough effort is invested in building the team. Actually, it is more reasonable to expect that we won't have a good team.

The following formula should explain this to you:

We can look at the(*) **actual team ability** as the result of the **potential team ability** less the **negative influences, powers and processes** that are happening in the team.

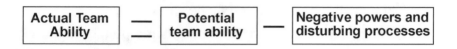

| Actual Team Ability | — — | Potential team ability | — | Negative powers and disturbing processes |

In this chapter we will first recognize the disturbing or helpful processes for the building and functioning of a team. We will discuss the processes that can lead to partial loss or to actualize the team potential. We will learn how to diminish or cancel the disturbing processes and how to strengthen the constructive process. **Building the team is mainly the task of the coach, but it is important that every single player in the team is aware of the personal influence he has on the team ability. Because of this, the chapter is important for every player.**

The behavior of the players in a team is different in a few aspects from the behavior of a single player. A good example for this came from an experiment 50 years ago(*). In it a group of people was checked with an instrument called a power-meter (an instrument that measures with the help of a spring and a meter the power that a man can pull) and their results were recorded. In the second stage of the experiment two participants were asked to measure their strength together and later groups of 3,4,5 people did the same. They all were asked to pull with their maximum strength.

(*)   Based on Steiner(1972) model .Steiner, I. (1972). **Group Process and Productivity** .New-York: Academics Press.

In all the cases when the participants were not alone it was found that they invested less power than the sum of the power when each of them pulled alone.

Later a few more experiments replicated these results, including a situation in which the participants did not see each other but were only told that others were pulling at the same time.

The simple knowledge that more people are pulling together led to the decline in invested energy and effort by the single participant even when he did not see the other people.

This example is a good illustration of what can happen in sport: the combined ability of the players in the team can be less than the sum of their personal abilities.

Why it happens?

As we said, human behavior in groups is different from our behavior when we are alone. It is true in a lot of spheres of life and is especially valid in sports in which the team is of great importance.

Step 10 :Execute your personal and team roles in every game and throughout the game.

If we go back to the experiment of pulling the spring and we imagine a good and united team participating in this experiment, every player who is pulling the spring together with the rest of his teammates will try harder than when he pulls alone.

(*)**The Ringelmann Effect** , in : Ingham A.G, Levinger,G, Graves,J , Peckham, V. (1974). The **Ringelmann Effect: Studies of Group Size and Group Performance**. Journal of Experimental Social Psychology. 10, 371-384.

The thought of the player should be "Now my effort influences the whole team and I must invest more". If all the players think like that we will have a situation in which their composite effort will be bigger than the sum of the effort each of them invested alone.

How to prevent and neutralize disturbing processes and negative forces and how to strengthen positive processes and powers?

1. Division of Responsibility

The team players feel sometimes that because the responsibility is shared by many of the players their personal responsibility as players is lower.

How this shows on the field?

A player tells himself "I will save my power and next attack I won't come back to defense, there are enough players in defense. Another player will take the responsibility and will cover me." It doesn't sound too bad when we speak about one attack only, but the problem is that the player does not coordinate his behavior with the rest of the players and it happens that in the same attack 2 or 3 players decide not to come back, because each of them thought that "It's not so bad, there are enough players". In this way a lot of goals are scored.

The problem is that the damage is not only the goal scored, but also the collective mood. The other players of the team are influenced by what just happened and it can lead to a significant damage to the team play. The feeling of dispersed responsibility expresses itself in the tendency to take bigger risks compared to a state of personal responsibility. In this way we can see a back defender taking the ball and advancing with it in attack (when this is against the instructions of the coach), or on a free kick, against the instructions, a player abandoning defense and heading for the ball.

When the professional team does not stress personal responsibility, the team can feel that everybody is responsible, or in other words that nobody is responsible.

Possible courses of action:

- The topic should be discussed with the team and it should be kept in awareness.
- The responsibility of every player should be stressed.
- It is advisable to capture on video examples of allowing goals because of badly coordinated responsibility and taking unnecessary risks. At the same time, good actions must be stressed in which personal responsibility leads the player to perform actions that are good for the team.
- The coaching staff must have a heavy hand over the players who don't keep their personal responsibility towards the team and encourage and reward cases of distinct personal responsibility without any connection to the result.

2. Dividing Effort

A similar thing happens with the effort invested. Exactly like in the experiment of pulling the spring meter, **the knowledge that the effort divides between several players leads us to not invest our maximum effort.**

Again, if we speak about a singe player, it is not so bad. The problem is exactly like in the experiment when the same thought exists in several players. The effort they invest declines and accordingly so does the team ability.

Possible courses of action:
- The topic should be discussed with the team and it should be kept in awareness.
- The importance of investing the maximum effort of every single player should be stressed - from the opening whistle to the end and without any dependency on the score or on the effort the other players invest.
- It is recommended to show the players examples on video of allowing goals because of players who do not invest effort.
- The coaching staff must have a heavy hand over the players who do not invest their personal effort towards the team and at the same time encourage and reward players who show distinct personal effort without any connection to the result.

3. The "Catastrophe" Effect

When players don't meet their personal responsibility and don't invest their maximum effort and in addition are not in their best shape (for any reason) **the result might be the breakdown of the whole team.**

Sometimes it is enough that in a specific game there are 2 or 3 players not in a good shape who do not keep their personal responsibility and do not invest the needed effort – and this can lead to the collapse of the whole team.

Sometimes, a team can neutralize the bad shape of players by investing extra effort covering for them, correcting their mistakes and encouraging them. This however, while not hurting the team ability, will eventually lead to the breakdown of the team.

The collapse of the team will happen when such players in addition to showing bad ability, won't take on the personal responsibility and won't invest effort in the game. Such behavior is "contagious".

A different possibility is that other players from the team might lose their belief in the team's ability to win in the game. Then their motivation will drop, the effort invested in the game will decline ("Why try harder if the others don't and lose every ball") and the team will break down.

In other words, instead of being in a position in which only a couple of players are not in good shape, but the team is functioning, fighting and investing effort we find ourselves in a total breakdown - a catastrophe.

Possible courses of action:

- You should bring the topic to the awareness of the players and talk about such situations in the team forum.
- In case there are examples from the games it is advisable to screen them on video.
- You should emphasize to the players the need for personal responsibility and investing maximum effort in every game the whole game, without any relation to their ability in the particular match.
- On the contrary, if their ability is declining you should ask them to show greater responsibility and especially greater effort in the team game and encouraging the other players
- You must make it clear that the players as professionals

must first of all take personal responsibility and invest their own effort, with no connection to what the rest of the players do. It is true that it is hard, frustrating and sometimes ineffective. However, if most of the players in the team act in this way, not only won't the team break down, it will be possible to win games, even when some of the players are not in a good shape.

4. "The Convenience Effect"

Players and teams can get into a state that I call "**the convenience effect**". Your team leads 2:0 in the 60th minute. The victory can be seen on the horizon and the whole team feels good and safe with the score. The impression is that the opponent cannot score a goal.

From this moment on the invested effort is lowered, the intensity and the determination become lower and the players enter a state of "the convenience effect" that usually leads quickly to the "catastrophe effect". Suddenly, the opponent team scores a goal and the team switches from a state of convenience to a state of stress. In such a moment the team should go to a higher gear and this is not always possible. **The result of such a situation is that a sure victory has turned to a draw or loss**.

Possible courses of action:
- You should bring the topic to the awareness of the players and talk about such situations in the team forum.
- Every single player must be aware of the tendency to decrease effort when the victory seems promised and to work against it. He should increase the effort

and encourage the rest of the players to increase their effort too.

- The coaching staff must encourage the players to not let the team to go down to a state of "convenience effect".

5. <u>Lack of equality in the team</u>

A soccer team will never be a team in which all the players are equal. In every team, the value of each player is different and the press coverage too. The rewards the players receive are not the same, the fans do not treat all the players in the same way and sometimes even the coaching staff and the management don't regard the players equally. A player who feels for a long time that he is the victim of injustice (real or imagined) won't be able to invest his maximum effort in the game. As a result, his concentration will be hurt as well as his self-confidence and thoughts like "why is it important to try harder and invest if nobody appreciates me?" will enter his mind and disturb him. This player won't play to his personal potential.

Possible courses of action:

- The coaching staff and the management must stick to an equal relationship with all the players on the team. This should include the duties and rights, improper behavior, being late etc. (fines and punishments) and in particular everything related to criticism and praise. The criticism should be faced only inside the team.

- Players salary must be confidential.

- Rewards over the pay must be the same. You cannot give a special premium to a player who scored a goal or to a goalkeeper who excelled in a specific game. Every bonus must be equal to all the players.

- Media coverage influences the players a lot. The press, in its nature, highlights the scorer and ignores the contribution of the other players. In this way, the press concentrates on the goalkeeper's mistake that led to the goal and overlooks all the mistakes of the forwards who failed to score.

In order to reduce the damage the press causes, the team must have a clear and unequivocal policy about the press and require its players to follow the policy. I don't believe in team restrictions to interview, but the opposite situation of total freedom of speech and every player telling the press what he wants and when he wants is also unacceptable.

I personally advise to give the right of speech to every player after each game on one condition: that the player will speak only about himself, will state explicitly the contribution of the whole team and won't pass criticism about the players or the coaching staff. More extensive interviews in the press can be done with the permission of the management and the coaching staff. The team must encourage the coverage of players who are not "stars" and to regulate in this way the coverage of the "stars". As a policy the players who enter the press conference should be those who in the eyes of the coaching staff gave most to the team in the specific game and not the player who did nothing the whole game but scored a goal in the last minute.

- When appearing in the media the management and coaching staff of the team should keep to the same policy. In other words, they should criticize themselves only and talk about others and the team only in positive terms.

6. <u>Blurring the importance of the single player.</u>

You cannot reach a state in which the emphasis on the team will blur the importance and contribution of the single player. When the players begin to feel that their unique contribution to the team is not valued and is not expressed publicly, this will lead to lowering their motivation.

This means that stressing equality is not enough and you need to find a way to strengthen the uniqueness of every player and the importance of his support for the team success.

Possible courses of action:

- You should give positive feedback to the effort of players. The feedback must be personal and public.
- The coaching staff should build a schedule of personal meetings with all the players through the whole season and not only when there are problems or need for criticism. The content of the meeting should be kept secret.
- The coaching staff must find a way to stress the contribution of a player even when it is hard to notice. For example, if this is a mediocre player who performs his duty with loyalty. It is possible to note him as a good example of a player who follows the instructions of the coach and follows the tactical discipline, as a player who contributes with his mental strength, encourages the team etc. You don't have to invent things, but in cases like this you should be creative and give the player the positive feedback he deserves.
- You must insist that the players encourage each other and react only in a positive way to every attempt another

player from the team made even if it is a failure or a mistake.

It is not important how angry a player is over his team mate or how sure he is they were wrong, the only intention you have after it happened is to encourage them, to emphasize the importance of the attempt and to go on. We will talk about this topic in detail later, but what I mean is: a situation in the game, when a player passes you the ball and it is not precise or he kicks the ball to somebody else or he waits too long and loses it. Your reaction as a player **must be positive**, instead of assaulting him with hurting curses/ yelling/ gestures etc. If you are close to the player, you can tell him something like: "Good thought. Next time!" And if you are far from him give him a sign of support – as recognition for the effort. You can clap hands for a second, raise a hand or a finger or even smile at him.

If you have the opportunity to exchange a couple of words with the player who in your eyes made a mistake or was wrong in not passing you the ball, you can remark in a sentence like: "Great try! Try to pay attention when I'm making a move and I'm free for the ball. Come on! Let's win this game!" Every reaction in this style will be more effective than many of the expressions of anger and yelling. If you are sure in your remarks, keep them for the game analysis on video when the team is gathered after the game. Then you will be able to express your opinion without anger and to explain your arguments for the places and situations in which the players made mistakes, didn't pass the ball, etc.

7. Emphasizing the score

When the professional team and all the people surrounding it **turn the score of the games into the only important thing, the road to the breakdown of the team is usually short.**
In sport it is impossible to concentrate only on the score.
Very often the score does not depend only on the team. A team can play with its full potential and still lose, because it played against a better team or because of a single mistake of a player, judgment error etc.

It is far more important, at least for the coaching staff and the players, to concentrate on the **team interaction** during the game. It's important to pay attention to the things that are under the **exclusive control** of the players and the coaching staff. For example, did the team prepare properly, did every player prepare physically and mentally for the game, did every player follow the instructions of the coach, did the players invest maximum effort throughout the game etc. Of course the team wants to win every game but it is impossible.

FOCUSING ON THINGS THAT ARE IN YOUR CONTROL WILL CONTRIBUTE TO THE TEAM MORE THAN CONCENTRATING ONLY ON THE SCORE!

Possible courses of action:
- It is true that the media/the fans and sometimes even the members of the management look only at the score and this is their right.
- A steady routine of behavior in the club after a game should be determined, without any dependency on the score. The steady behavior must cover all areas.
- Part of the routine should be the **professional**

analysis of the last game. Again, after a loss and especially after a victory (even if it is easier to correct mistakes and criticize after a victory than after a loss).

- The emphasis in the analysis must be on the actions that were under the control of the team and the coaching staff.

It will not help if the team agrees it had bad luck or that the referees were against them. Emphasizing areas that are not under the control of the team will eventually lead to damage to the team.

8. Creating sub-groups in the team

During the activity of the team sub-groups of different kinds can be created. In fact there is nothing wrong with sub-groups if they do not disturb the team's functioning and if their goals are identical to the team goals.

The problem is when sub-groups arise in order to solve problems common only to the members of the sub-group. When these problems are expressed in practice or during the game, the team ability is hurt substantially. These are some examples of sub-groups that can exist in a team:

- Foreign players
- Young players
- Players from the bench
- Personal friends
- Groups of players with close duties (like defenders) etc.

How is this expressed in practice and in the game?

When a sub-group acts as a separate team the players of

the group will prefer their own goals, in other words put their personal interests before the team goals. In such situations they will prefer to pass the ball first to the members of the sub-group. The first option to pass the ball is to someone from the sub-group and only if this is impossible to give the ball to somebody else. The interest is of course to improve one's status within the sub-group.

In the same way, when a player makes a mistake or when he needs help or needs to be covered the members of the sub-group will do it for their friends from the sub-group but will be reluctant to help the rest of the players.

Examples from the field:

- In one team there was a sub-group of foreign players. During the first half of the season there was no expression of the sub-group in practice or on the field. However, with the end of the first round approaching, with rumors starting about exchanging one of the foreign players, the rest of the foreigners began passing him most of the balls in order to strengthen his position in the team. And because this was not always the best pass option this created serious bitterness in the rest of the players and the team functioning was hurt.

- In another team there was a sub-group of personal friends. When one of them experienced loss in ability and the coach hinted that he would take him out of the line-up his friends from the sub-group tried to pass him most of the balls and when he made a mistake they tried harder to correct it. In interviews with the media, the friends tried to bring out the importance of the player and did the same with the professional team. Very quickly the functioning of the team was hurt.

- The young players in a team felt they were treated unfairly and did not receive enough opportunities. Every time two or more young players were in the line-up they tried to help each other, even when this hurt the team.

The formation of sub-groups in a team is natural but it is forbidden to reach a situation in which the members of the sub-group will prefer their goals before the team or the situation in which the functioning of the subgroup inside the team damages the team game.

Possible courses of action:

- The players must be conscious about the subject and it should be aware of the damage to the team. The professional staff must be attentive to this subject and recognize the formation of sub-groups as early as possible.
- You should act directly to disperse sub-groups in training. This means that when small groups practice, you must be careful to break down sub-groups. It is important that not all the foreigners, the bench players, etc. play together.
- You must treat in word and deed all the players as individuals and not according to their membership in a sub-group. You must call the players by personal name and not with an inclusive name like the "foreign players" or the "young" etc. Also when you want to praise the players, you must mention their names and not something like "Take a lesson from the foreigners…"
- You have to strengthen each and every player's personal identity and importance for the team.

- If all these actions don't help and the situation is that the sub-group hurts the whole team, you must act with determination and if necessary expel the players from the team.

9. The bench players

In professional team sports, very often the final result of a game and of the whole season is determined by the replacements.

In every team during the whole season, players must be replaced and the opportunity will be given to the bench players to prove themselves in the starting line-up. Everybody agrees with that, but what actually happens is that the coaches and mainly the team management don't give the needed importance to this subject.

The bench players can build the team success, but they can also cause the destruction of the team.

When the bench players become a consolidated sub-group, their preferences can become opposite to the team goals. There were enough cases in which bench players became opposition to the coach and acted to replace him, even though that when they were fitted in the game they didn't give a thing to the team and sometimes even drew the team back.

When the bench players are embittered and lacking motivation, there is tension inside the team. This tension hurts the motivation of the other players, does not allow the training to be efficient and eventually weakens the team.

The right work with the bench players is essential for the team success. On the other hand, insufficient investment in

these players is a certain way to team failure.

You must distinguish between the players sitting on the bench. This group is made up of a couple of players who only intend to train with the team in order to fill up the team. These are usually young or new players.

These players must be aware that in this stage they are in the team to train and improve and in the future they will be fitted to the team. However, for now they are not entering the line-up.

I will say it again, **there should be no misunderstanding about this.**

The second part of the bench are those who are capable of replacing the line-up, but because of professional considerations they don't start. **You must treat these players exactly like you treat those of the starting line-up.**

Possible courses of action:

- You must talk about the status of the bench players and the subject must be clear to all the players (a starting player today can sit on the bench tomorrow).
- The coaching staff must make sure that the bench players understand that they are on the bench only because of professional considerations.
- **A bench player must understand that his way back to the starting line-up depends on his investment in training, on demonstrating ability when replacing a player, but also on the decline of ability of the player he replaces (injury, red card, sickness, loss of fitness). In other words, not everything depends on him.**
- The professional team must practice in training with different line-ups, integrating bench players with the first

team.

- The professional team should treat the bench player personally and not as a group. Every bench player must know why he is sitting and what he has to do in order to return to the line-up.
- During training you must treat the bench players **exactly** like the starting players in terms of discipline, training instructions, sticking to the training program, etc.
- The coaching staff must be sensitive and prevent situations in which the bench players become a united team inside the team.

For soccer players who find themselves on the bench for any reason:

As we said, it is easy to get out of the starting team, but it is much harder to come back. Blaming the whole world because it does not appreciate your ability and becoming an opposition against the coaching staff, will not help you get back into the line-up.

You must understand that you must do everything that depends on you in order to return to the line-up. This means to train the best you can and when you get in the game to prove yourself.

Also, you must be aware that not everything depends on you. If the player starting in your position is showing better ability than you, it doesn't matter how good you are in the training you won't return to the line-up. You should be patient, work hard and wait.

It is true that it is difficult to prepare for a game when you are not a part of the starting team, but you must invest all the effort. The mental preparation for a game should be for you as if you are starting the game.

While you are sitting on the bench, you are not a spectator or a fan. You must be in the game and concentrate on a player or the players you might replace. Think what are their problems are and what might work better.

When you are asked to warm up, you must prepare mentally at the same time.

During the warm up, take deep breaths and visualize the game. Regulate your stress and your motivation. Work on your self-confidence and on the belief in your ability. All this without any connection to the time you have to play.

Don't waste the chance in anger over the coach who lets you only now into the game. The anger will only disturb you and will prove to the coach that he was right from the beginning, when he didn't put you in the starting line-up.

When you enter the game:
- Don't try immediately to perform an action that needs a lot of concentration or has little chance of success.
- Start with simple and efficient moves.
- Enter the game gradually, perform the instructions of the coaching staff and reflect on your conclusions about the mistakes the player you replaced made.
- In any case, give your team the feeling that they can trust you. Encourage, push forward and play aggressively (but not wildly).
- Concentrate on the present game and in every single

action. Don't think about the importance of the game: - "What will happen if we lose?" or "Will I return to the line-up if I have a good game?". Thoughts like these will only disturb you. Concentrate on the present. You can think after the game. Remember that players more famous than you (and much more expensive) sat or will sit on the bench in one or another stage of their career.

The wisdom is to be patient, to take the bench as a part of the game and to work hard to return to the line-up.

If in two years you don't succeed in entering the line-up of the team you play with, it is time to make decisions and choose another team.

You must start playing even if it means moving to a lower league. If you do not play for a long time, you lose your skill and won't have the chance to prove yourself.

It is better to play in the starting line-up of a lower team and prove yourself.

Do not agree to be the permanent replacement.
This is the way to the end of your career!

10. Placing goals in front of the team

I mentioned earlier that one of the basic conditions for the consolidation of a team is the common goal. The subject of placing goals in sport is important for the team and the single player and I will treat the subject in chapter 15.

In order for a team to stick together it must have a clear and common goal. The emphasis is on common. In other words all the members of the team (it is important that it is common to the players, the professional staff, the owners, the management, the doctor and everybody else who has a role in the team) must agree with the team goals and believe in the possibility of achieving them.

Goals can build the team, but they can ruin it too.

When the goals are unclear and especially when they are not uniform this can lead to damage for the team. In other words, when the owner has different ideas from the goals of the coach or a situation in which the coach and the players don't have the same objectives the team will be hurt. Additional damage might be done if the players do not believe that the goals in front of them are achievable.

Possible courses of action:

- The professional team must declare realistic goals before the beginning of the season. It must be certain that the goals are accepted by the management/owners etc.

In soccer there were some cases in which the coaching staff formulated the team goals together with the management, but the management expected to achieve much more and, to no one's surprise, after a few losses there was a crisis in the team, coach's dismissal etc.

- The players must participate in defining the goals
- In any case, after the goals are set, you should work on the common belief of everyone, that it is possible to achieve the goals.
- **Goals are not sacred** and sometimes it is necessary to update and formulate them from the beginning, again with everybody's approval. It is clear that there is no sense when the team is lagging significantly behind the first team of the table to continue talking about the championship as the only possible goal. Being stubborn about

goals in which the players do not believe not only promises their failure, but also very often may lead to the failure of the whole team. This does not mean that I advise to giving up. If the realistic goal that was placed in front of the team was to win the championship and for different reasons now the team is far from the possibility to achieve this goal (though it is still theoretically possible), you have to formulate the goal from the beginning. For example, to gain as many possible points from the games left to guarantee second place in the league and more.

- Every player in every game must have a personal goal. These goals are given by the coach or by the player himself. The personal performance is important to every player beyond the team game. His general goal should be to disturb the game of the player he plays against in defense and attack (we deal with personal goals later in the book) and to execute the coach's instructions.

11. Team Cohesion

One of the subjects on which there is no agreement is how important the team cohesion for the team success. There were teams whose players stuck together and were friends and the team succeeded and there were exactly the opposite cases, in which the relationships between the players were excellent but the team did not function. In professional soccer there are many teams in which the players cannot stand each other personally and the team succeeds.

As a principle you must distinguish between social welding and goal consolidation – the latter for achieving common

goals. Apparently, in soccer the goal consolidation is more important.

It is not to say that all the players have to be friends and spend time together after training, but a certain degree of social welding is essential for success.

Possible courses of action:

- You must keep the subject in awareness, speak about it and distinguish between friendships and consolidating to achieve a goal.
- You must encourage actions that strengthen the social welding - common pastime, dinners etc.
- In the training camp you must give the players an assignment to learn about each other. You may order the players to invest half an hour every day talking with the player they know the least, talking about soccer and personal things.
- The coaching staff must be constantly watchful to recognize processes that hurt the social unity and the goal consolidation.
- It is important to create team pride and to emphasize the uniqueness of the team compared to other teams. For this it is important to have an emblem, color for the outfit and every other unique sign.
- It is important to create a motto for the club like "We play for the club"

Summary

In this chapter I dealt with different aspects of the team formation and preservation. As I said, the coaching staff is responsible for the creation of the team, but it is important that every player knows these processes and will invest his best for the team success. Because there is no taste to the personal success if it is not followed by at least some team success.

- As a player in a team you have personal responsibility for its success.
- You must exceed in your personal role, but also in your team role.
- Your actions as a member of the team can either build it or ruin it.
- Think always of the consequences of your actions (words and deeds) for the team.
- The understanding of the team processes as explained in this chapter will make you a better player.
- Bench players must adopt the way of work I offered.

The Coach Box

The fact that a group of talented players train together for a long time is not enough to turn them into a good team. Beyond this, your personal belief about how a team is created, the topics that were present in this chapter are important for the success of the team. In every topic of these subjects the first line is – bring the subject to awareness and talk about it openly. That is your duty.

The training camp is the place where most of the work for consolidating the team must be done and you must be careful that it does not turn into a test camp. The players on the team should be agreed in its better part before entering the training camp. A good time to choose the players and organize the training camp is at the end of the season.

Building a team is a process that never ends.
It is your duty to invest thought and time to the
subject the whole season.

Your personality and temperament as a coach determine your style of work with the team, but you must deal with most of the topics we discussed even if in your opinion they are not important.

We must agree on one thing – the players do not need you as a friend. They have enough friends. They need you as a leader to help them achieve their goals.

I offer you and the team again, to accept the slogan: (especially if you have in your team players who think they are stars or the press treats them in this way)

Stars shine only in the sky!
And even in the sky they are arranged in groups!

You cannot expect a team game from
a bunch of players.
You need a team for a team game.

Chapter 14 – Motivation and Sport

Everybody thinks they know what motivation is. Everybody speaks about it, blames it for his failures and praises it when he wins. However, motivation, like most of the things connected with human behavior, is a complex term.

In this chapter I will bring the subject to proportion. You will learn how to recognize your level of motivation and how to regulate it.

Most of the people dealing with sport believe that motivation is like money – the more you have the better. In sport, the relation between motivation, ability and success is much more complex.

If you ask me to run 60 meters (why only 60 meters, surely he can't run more) the fastest I can (with the soul of a sportsman I will surely agree) I suppose that I will take them in 11 seconds. If you tell me that if I run again and succeed in improving the result you will give me $1000, I'm sure I will better the time (if I manage to reach the end).

If you tell me then that if I run again and improve the time once more I will receive one million dollars, what will happen? Will I improve the time?

Most certainly I won't, because on the one hand I've reached the maximum of my ability and on the other the pressure and stress will hurt my ability. In other words, even if I try with all my strength, with all my heart to improve the time (and I will have record motivation), I won't make it.

Increasing motivation does not necessarily lead to improvement in ability.

In the example, money was the source of motivation.
**Does money lie in the basis of motivation
in sport as well?**

**In professional sport everyone plays for money.
However, money is not enough to guarantee motivation.**

In every soccer training – it is enough to bet on a can of soda and immediately the motivation of the players rises and the game becomes much more intense. This means that it is not so simple and that not only money influences motivation. **All of us know teams whose players did not receive salary for several months and still they defeated teams who pay their players every month.**

What is Motivation?

Motivation can be defined as the desire or need that makes the person act in order to achieve his goals.

This definition makes clear the connection between motivation and placing goals and because of the importance of the subject I will deal with placing goals in sport in more detail than in the previous chapter.

The relation between the level of motivation and ability is not simple. It is close to the relation between stress and ability and the following figure illustrates this:

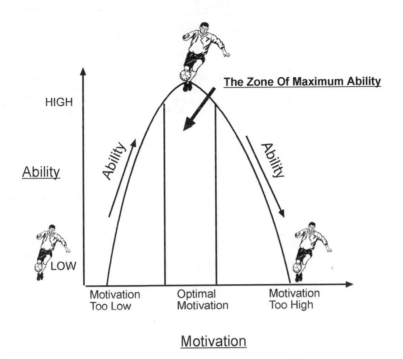

The Zone Of Maximum Ability

HIGH

Ability

Ability

Ability

LOW

Motivation
Too Low

Optimal
Motivation

Motivation
Too High

Motivation

Let's check now the meanings of this example. The drawing expresses in fact the complex connection between the ability on the field and motivation.

Every athlete has a field in which with the rise of his motivation his ability also gets better, until it reaches a level of motivation that leads the player to achieve his maximum performance.

When motivation continues to grow more than this level there will be a drop in ability.

This means that it is possible that two players will be at the same level of motivation, but its influence on their ability will be completely different. For the first one it can be the needed level for maximum performance, yet for the second it can be a level too high or too low from the motivational level he needs.

The goal of every player should be the right recognition of his level of motivation before the game. He must know the level of motivation that allows him to reach maximum ability and how to regulate his motivation in order to bring it to the desirable level for best performance.

How can it be that too much motivation lowers ability instead of increasing it?

When the level of motivation is too high, the pressure rises and concentration is hurt and this leads to lower ability. High motivational levels have immediate expression on the players' behavior on the field as well. A player with excess motivation will likely make aggressive fouls and will receive a yellow or red card. Such a player might invest too much effort in the beginning of the game and won't be able to "finish" it.

The combination between excess motivation and mistakes leads to frustration and the result:

The player really wants to but in fact he doesn't succeed!!!

What is the source of motivation?

I believe that in sport motivation must come **from the player** and not from **outside** factors.

What actually stands as the source of motivation (other than money) is the desire and the urge of the player to be the best in the sport he plays and to show his best ability!

In psychology we call this "self-actualization".

The desire and urge of the player to be the best has the power and a goal. That's why when working on motivation you must concentrate on its power and direction. When you

are conscious of your ability to regulate the intensity and direct yourself towards achieving goals, you will be able to regulate your level of motivation to fit your maximum ability.

A soccer player whose motivation depends on external factors such as the coach, the owners of the team, the mayor (I don't think that in London the mayor enters Arsenal's changing room before an important game to give motivation to the players – this is an Israeli invention), the army general (another Israeli invention) the press or other factors like these according to the team – **is a player in trouble. The main source of motivation must come from the player!**

Step 11: Take personal responsibility for the motivational level best suited to your potential

A mentally strong player knows how to enter every game and competition with the motivational level fitting his maximum ability and he knows how to keep and regulate his motivation along the whole game. This is the only way to explain Michael Jordan's ability in basketball, Pete Sampras' in tennis or Maradona's (in his best days) in soccer.

In modern soccer, there are just a few players who are capable of keeping their motivation steady and matching their maximum ability.

(name 2-3 players in your country)

Why did I mention only a couple of players?

Soccer players are only human beings. The demand to keep a level of motivation for a long period of time is extremely hard for every athlete and especially in team sports.

Here are some factors that influence the motivation and make it difficult for the player to keep it at the desired level for a long time:

- The connection between the players and the team influences the personal motivation of every player. It is very difficult for the single player to play with maximum motivation when the rest of the team is playing without motivation and does not invest in the game.

- It is enough that a couple of players from the team don't play with their maximum motivation to lower the motivation of the other players. In such situations this tendency of lowering motivation is a result of thoughts like: "Why should I make an effort when the others don't care" or "I kill myself to win the ball and they lose it indifferently" or "I'm the only one working hard, what a pity".

- **To give up and fit your motivational level to the other players is an easy solution, but such decision can hurt the team and you personally** (see the "catastrophe effect" from the previous chapter).

So what we do?

You are the only one responsible for your motivation. You have no excuses. You must continue to invest, try harder, fight and keep your level of motivation all along the game, without being dependent on the other players.
The responsibility is all yours.

If every player in the team thinks this way even when some of the players, for any reason, play with low motivation the damage to the team won't be significant.

When you think that the others do not have motivation the right way to behave is to give personal example and to invest effort encouraging and pushing the other players. **Coordinate** with the coaching staff, wait for the first opportunity and when the team is together start a conversation about the subject. **Remember the easy solution is to give up, to stop trying is very tempting but this is not the way**.

THE MOTIVATION IS YOURS; DON'T BLAME OTHERS IF IT DECLINES!

As I said, the goal is to start every game with a level of motivation best suited to your maximum ability, and keep it throughout the whole game.

Factors such as the opponent or the score should not influence you. However, we are only human and our basic inclination is to be influenced by the situation. Every player knows that there are no problems with motivation when playing against the champions, the leading team of the league or any other respected team.

The problem with motivation arises in games against the "weak" teams, against teams from the lower leagues in the National Cup Games, or on the contrary against teams that we have never defeated, against teams that we do not stand a chance etc.

One more factor influencing motivation is **the score during the game**. Players tend to lower their motivation when they see a close victory or when it looks like they don't have a chance.

What do we do?

Again, you are the only one responsible for your motivation and nothing about the team you are playing against or the score should lower your motivation. The responsibility is all yours.

If you learn to concentrate on yourself, only on the level of motivation that helps you show your maximum ability, there will be no influence by the other factors on you.

How can you know the level of motivation fitting your maximum ability?

Build yourself a "motivation meter" (similar to your stress meter) and with its help learn to measure your motivational level. Recollect previous games and check what was your motivation before them. Remember your good games in which you excelled with maximum ability and try to capture the level of motivation before the game.

If you work on this for a while, with time you will learn to estimate your motivational level and to recognize what is the motivation that fits you.

Many studies on athletes have found two important personality characteristics that influence motivation in competitive sport:

- The fear of losing
- The need for achievement

To fear losing is the way you see your chances of defeat. No athlete loves to lose, but still a defeat influences different players in different ways and in this way influences motivation too.

The need for achievement is our level of competitiveness. The way you are looking actively for challenge in competitions. Every athlete strives towards achievements, but everyone's urge for success has a different level of intensity.

It is accepted to distinguish between 4 types of people:

- People who have a low need for achievement and a high level of fear of losing. **If you are dealing with sport, you are certainly not from this type of person**.
- People who have a low need for achievement and a low level of fear of losing. Again people involved with competitive sport won't be from this type. These are people who do not understand what other people find in sport.
- People with a high need for achievement and low fear of losing. It is possible that you belong to this type. **Most players belong to this group**. Such people love competition and know how to accept defeat. As athletes, they do not have any problem with motivation in their games. They do have difficulty in investing motivation in training for a long period of time.
- People with a high need for achievement, but also with a high fear of losing. Some players belong to this category. **Such athletes love competition but a loss is problem atic for them. They lose their self-confidence and the belief in their ability. They are afraid to take risks during the game, run away from responsibility and the fear of losing paralyzes them**. As athletes these people will not succeed in finding their potential.

Try to check where you belong. Be sincere with yourself. Think how strong your need for success is and how strong your fear of losing.

If you have difficulty placing yourself in one of these categories it is completely normal. You are simply situated in the middle.

Study yourself and if your fear of losing is strong it is possible and necessary to change it. It's true that you can try to change alone, but it is recommended to seek assistance from a sport psychologist. **In any case, the first step is to get to know yourself and to understand that what you are influences your motivation and helps or hinders you in expressing your real ability.**

An additional factor influencing motivation is the presence of a leader on the field. **A team leader can be the major factor for keeping the team level of motivation**. A leader in sport is a player from the team who is trusted by the other players and they believe in his ability. The team believes that when the ball is with him something good is going to happen. (He is not necessarily the captain. The ideal situation is that the leader is the captain as well). **A leader for me is a player who reacts exactly the opposite of the other players**. When everybody is celebrating after scoring a goal he is trying to calm down, organize and continue to play. In the same way, when everyone is desperate after allowing a goal, he is encouraging, calming the players and pushing them to continue. When everyone is desperate and willing to give up the game he drives the players forward and demands they continue and believe in a possible good result. Even when only a few minutes are left to the end of the game and everyone is tired and waiting for the game to end, he pushes, encourages and demands from all of the players to fight till the end, to the final whistle.

A team with such a leader is on the way to success, at least in everything related to keeping the motivation level.

Even when there is a leader and especially when there isn't, still the responsibility for **your** motivation lies always on you as a player. When there is a leader you must help him, join him, strengthen him and be an example for the other players. When a leader is missing, the responsibility of every player is to be a **leader** in his part of the field. If you are a forward, try to be a leader in attack, if you are a defender – be a leader in defense.

When the team doesn't have a leader that everybody trusts, but a couple of players take partial responsibility, their influence on the team can be substantial in a lot of areas and in particular on **motivation**.

Because of the special importance of the team goals on motivation; the following chapter deals more closely with the goals in soccer.

Summary

- Only you are responsible for your level of motivation. There is no excuse.
- The major source of motivation must be inside of you and not an outside factor.
- Know what personal factors influence your motivation.
- Recognize the outside reasons that influence your motivation.
- **Your goal is to start every game with a level of motivation best suited for your maximum ability, and keep it through the whole game, from the opening whistle to the final one.**

The Coach Box

The motivation of the players and the team is important for success.

As I said, players are only human and every player is a different man. There is no one level of motivation that fits the maximum ability of most of the players from the team and that's why it is impossible to work on the motivation of all the players together.

The level of motivation the team will reach can fit the

maximum ability of some of the players, but it can also lead the rest of them to a too high motivational level in relation to the level fitting their maximum ability.

The result of entering the team into a "frenzy" before the game is not necessarily positive. You must work on motivation inside the team, but at the same time you must insist that all the players work on their motivation.

You must know the players and try to help them regulate the level of motivation. **It is your duty to emphasize to them that their motivational level is their personal responsibility and they should not trust any external factor to lead them to the desired level of motivation.**

It is your responsibility to know the right level of motivation of the players. You should demand from **all** the players **all the time** to work on their motivation.

Don't enter the trap of working on motivation only before "important" games. In games like these the players don't have problems with motivation. The problem usually lies in the "easy" and "not important" games.

As a coach you have the ability to influence motivation by placing goals and we will deal with this in the following chapter.

Chapter 15 –
Defining Your Goals – the Way to Success

Step 12: Define the right goals

Some of the people involved with sport and around it (especially a part of the journalists and the commentators) think that there is no such thing as goals in sport. For them sport has only one goal – and it is victory. Everybody knows the saying:

Victory is not the most important thing –
It is the only thing!

If you also think this way, we have a problem!

In sport there is always more than just a victory. It is true that in professional sport the goal is always to win and always to come in first place, but it is wrong if this is the only goal.

A soccer player whose only goal is victory won't be
capable of maintaining a high professional
level in sport for a long time.

Not a single athlete or team always wins. The loss is part of sport and you should know how to cope with it. **Not every loss is a failure**. When you have an additional goal besides victory it is still possible to lose, and still fulfill some of your goals and continue developing into a better player.

Beyond all these things, in sport the victory or the loss does not depend only on you, because you can compete against another team or player or you can reach your maximum ability – and still not win. **In soccer the team can play the best it can and**

still in some of the games it won't be enough to win.

That is why when we speak about goals in sport we distinguish between goals that depend only on us – **operational goals** like showing maximum ability, aggressive game, integrating the young players, team game, pressing the opponent or defensive play of the whole team etc. and goals that depend on our opponent as well – **achievement/result goals** like victory, scoring goals etc.

In some games the team will reach the operational goals, but won't attain the achievement goals. In cases like these, the team played a good game, but the other team played better and won.

In the previous chapters I spoke about goals from the team and motivational aspects. In this chapter I talk about defining personal goals in soccer. Because apart from placing goals in front of the team every player should define for himself (with the help of the coach) goals for every practice and every game, for several months, for the end of the season and for the more distant future.

Defining goals is the **foundation** on which motivation is built. The desire to fulfill your goal will give you a push when you are already exhausted. The goals will push you to continue playing and give whatever you can even when you are out of luck and the team is going to lose. Your goals will support you during the game to the final whistle, even when you don't win. However, you must learn to do this **right.**

Goals can push you forward, but mistakes in defining the goals or treating goals in the wrong way may be damaging.

Why do goals influence us?

- Goals sustain motivation for a long time.
- They help us determine what is really important for us. They will help us to put things in perspective, to concentrate on what is important for achieving the goals and to ignore the insignificant.
- Goals increase the effort. They push you forward to improve and be better.
- Goals help you concentrate. Defining goals makes it possible for you to concentrate on their achievement.
- The goals will lead you to learn new things in order to improve.
- Completing a goal is a positive reinforcement for you that will drive you to work to achieve the other goals too.
- Defining goals makes possible the recognition of the obstacles that lie on the way to completing the goals.
- Placing goals in practice as well will make them more efficient.

The goals are yours. They are meant to help you and advance you. Even if you need to consult with the team coaching staff, you are solely responsible for completing your goals.

You are also responsible for defining the goals and for investing the effort for their achievement.

Rules for the right definition of goals and for deriving the maximum benefit from the work on them:

- Where possible define **specific goals** that can be measured. Don't place general goals. A goal like improving your defensive play is too broad. You should prefer more strict and unequivocal formulation like: "From my side of the field not more than 5 goals will be scored this season" or "The mistakes I make in every game will be less than..." or "Improving coordination in defense". Sometimes when there is no way to formulate specific goals you can place goals like improving the offensive game, when it is clear to you what you intend (it does not necessarily mean scoring more goals, attack is more than scoring goals).
- Define hard goals, but **possible to complete**. Goals that are a **challenge for you**. You can define some comparatively easy goals as well for achieving on the first stage. However, most of your goals must be a challenge for you.
- Define goals in the long-term, middle term and short-term. A goal in the long-term can be to play in the national team, to play in a team abroad, to be chosen in the team of the year etc. Goals for the middle term include goals for the range of several months like – losing 5 lbs, improving sprint time to 12 seconds for 100 meters, becoming starter, etc. The goals in the short-term are relevant for the next training (yes, it is important to come with goals to every training) and the following game. The goals of the game will be formulated with the help of the coaching staff or by yourself alone (goals like: "I will guard...and he won't be a factor in this game", "I will have more than 80% success in my passes", "I will be aggressive" and certainly possible goals like: "I will help the captain in the team work" etc.).

- Define mainly goals for performance and not result /achievement. Of course, it is impossible to overlook these goals forever, but it is important to place additional performance goals like improving the percentage of successful passes, lessening the number of lost balls, putting pressure on the opponent, aggressive play, etc. Remember that you are **solely** responsible for the performance goals. These are goals that you can **always work** to achieve without any connection to the score. If your only goal is victory, when it seems to you that you won't win this game you stop playing. However, if your goal is to be aggressive or to put pressure on the other team you can continue and invest in these goals to the final whistle. In fact, **if you act this way in addition to the effort of the other players it can eventually lead to victory even from a situation that seems hopeless at first sight**. (Bayern against Manchester United in the final of the European Championship 1999).

- **Recognize the obstacles** that deny you the goals you have defined. The correct recognition of these difficulties will help you define more specific goals. For example, if you want to achieve an improvement in your defensive play the obstacle can be a lack of physical power or fitness. This means that you can place additional goals for yourself like improving your body fitness and power.

- Find the way or the strategy needed for fulfilling your goals. Check what you need to do to achieve your goals. If we continue with the previous example, in order to improve your physical power you decide for example to practice in the fitness room 3 times a week. If the goal is to improve your body fitness you can decide to stay after every training and continue working or you can run 10 km twice a week etc. **There is no sense in defining**

a goal that you have no idea what to do in order to achieve it.

- Write down your goals on a piece of paper. It is important to see the goals and formulate them on paper. Writing down the goals will assure that you define goals according to the instructions and not unclear goals that exist only in our mind and imagination. List as well the obstacles you expect on your way and check with yourself how you intend to overcome them.

- **Goals you have defined are not sacred**. It is possible to change and update them. It is clear to you that for various reasons if you do not succeed with the goals you have chosen after a certain period of time you will change them, fit them to reality or replace them with goals that can be achieved. **When you have fulfilled your goals your self-confidence will rise and you will feel satisfaction. This is the time when you will want to define new goals for yourself. In other words, when you advance according to your goals you are always "hungry" for success.**

Work on your goals!
This is a profitable investment.

It is important to emphasize that the goals are not our fantasies. Of course, there is nothing wrong with fantasies and only one who has fantasies has the potential to achieve them, but fantasies are out of place when we are talking about defining goals. Goals should be possible to achieve and fantasies need not meet this criterion.

Summary

- It is important to define goals for every training, every game, the following months and coming year.
- It is important to determine what is needed from you to achieve your goals and the obstacles on your way.
- It is important to formulate the goals according to the instructions and it is essential to have them written down.
- Before every game, you should be sure that you know what your goals in the game are and what you must do to succeed.
- Goals make you "hungry". They will sustain your motivational level for a long time.
- Achieving your goals gives you a lot of satisfaction and strengthens your self-confidence and the belief in your ability. Right after achieving a goal, congratulate yourself and define a new goal.

The Coach Box

I wrote about goals in a chapter that dealt with the team. The instructions for efficient goal definition that were present in this chapter are true for placing team goals as well.

As a coach, your duty is to require the players to define goals for themselves, to help them formulate the goals and to give them goals for the short term or in other words for the coming game.

Additionally, your duty is to evaluate how your players stand up to the goals they have defined for themselves and also to judge their progress towards achieving their mid and long term goals.

If you succeed in working with team and personal goals, you have solved a significant part of your team motivation problems.

Chapter 16 – A short break

If you have reached this part of the book you need a short break. You are now approximately in the middle of this book. This is a good time to take a rest and to drink a cup of coffee and this is also time to summarize for yourself what you have read up to now (yes, even at halftime your head must continue working. This is true when reading a book and it is certainly true in the halftime of the game). Check what this means to you. Look over and decide what you can implement and with what you disagree. Think, how would you mark yourself in the areas you read about up to now.

Take a couple of minutes with yourself.

Everything you read up to this point was meant to turn you into a better player – a player capable of expressing his real potential in the game.

If you want this to happen it is important to work regularly on all the areas I mentioned:
- Coping with stress and pressure.
- Mental preparation
- Visualization and defining goals.

When the game starts additional elements of your mental strength become active that can build you as a player or can prevent you from showing your real ability. I speak about the essence of mental strength:

Self-confidence and belief in ability
Emotional control
Concentration

The three following chapters will deal with these subjects. As a player you must be aware of the influence of any of these factors on your performance on the field.

Remember these elements and check with yourself during the game. Think, "What happens with my self-confidence?" and also "Do I control my emotions and concentration?". The smart thing is to recognize the changes while they are happening during the game. Only in this way is it possible to correct them. There is no sense sitting at the end of the game and reaching the conclusion that you were not concentrated and that is why you missed and made mistakes. It won't give you a thing. It is much more important to pay attention to what is happening in you during the game and to try to change it. In this way at the end of the game you won't need excuses like "If I was concentrated I could have scored" or "If I were in control of my emotions I would not have received the yellow card".

The components of mental strength do not work separately. On the contrary, they are dependent on each other and one is the result of the other the same way it is influenced by the third. When you do not control your emotions immediately your concentration will suffer and when you are not concentrated your self-confidence will decline.

Because all the elements of mental strength are essen-

tial for your success it is important that you are aware of their influence and are capable of regulating them to fit the state that allows you to show your full ability on the field.

Again, all the elements are essential. There is no use of self-confidence without concentration or emotional control. In such a situation the self-confidence does not have any support in reality and the result will be bad ability.

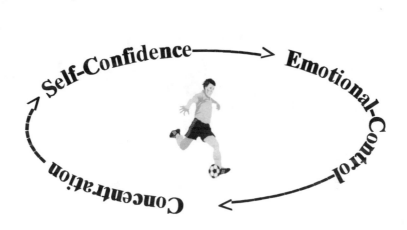

You have rested enough. It is time to continue reading the book.

Chapter 17 –
Self - confidence and belief in personal abilities

We can define self-confidence as the belief in your personal ability to perform an action or behavior successfully.

The essence of self-confidence is the **expectation to succeed**. Action or behavior can be either a specific kick or more generally showing your real ability during the whole game. This is the essence of self-confidence in a soccer game.

Self-confidence in soccer is the belief in your ability to play at your highest level throughout the game, without being influenced by the score, the opponent or the performance of the rest of the team.

It is important to emphasize that I do not speak about belief in victory. Of course, you want to win, however a win or a loss depends on a variety of factors and **you do not have control over them**. Your self-confidence depends only on you and because of that in principle it is based on the belief in your ability and not on the score of the game.

When a player starts to doubt his ability and thoughts like "Am I good enough?" or "Am I capable of guarding this player?" start to rise in his mind – this is the beginning of the road to failure.

The importance of the player's self-confidence

☺ As I said, the opposite of self-confidence is the doubt in your ability. We know today that the chance to succeed in every action you take, even the simplest one, depends on your belief in the ability to succeed. When you are preparing for a penalty kick and the thought "I won't score this time" enters your mind, the chances grow that this thought will fulfill itself and you really won't succeed. On the contrary, if the thought that you will score enters your mind, the chances that this will happen become greater.

Your belief in success is an essential condition for your victory.

(and this is not the only condition, as we will see later).

Self-confidence strengthens positive feelings. When you are sure in yourself the chances that you will control your feelings in states of stress are higher.

Self-confidence helps you concentrate better. When you are sure in yourself your thoughts can concentrate on the assignments in front of you. On the contrary, when you do not have confidence in yourself you will be dealing with thoughts of how to prevent failure and this will hurt your concentration.

Self-confidence allows aggressive, determined play. If you are certain of your success in every action you perform on the field, you will perform every action with determination and aggressiveness.

Your self-confidence allows you to define goals for yourself that are challenging and gives you the ability to act consistently and with determination to achieve these goals.

Your self-confidence makes you invest more. The time and quantity of effort you are ready to invest depend on your self-confidence. A player who believes in himself will be ready to invest more effort, when all the other players are tired and are waiting for the final whistle. Very often,

this effort can be the only difference between a win and a loss.

Your self-confidence influences your attitude about the game. When you are confident you play **to win**. On the contrary, when your self-confidence is missing you play **not to lose**. A player certain of himself is ready to try and also make mistakes, but most of the time his actions will be efficient for the team. A player lacking self-confidence is **afraid of mistakes** and at most his contribution to the team will be insignificant. When a player with confidence enters the game (as a replacement) he will try to act to change the game. On the other hand, if this is a player lacking self-confidence, he will only try not to make mistakes.

The problem is that when we concentrate on "How not to make mistakes", it is extremely difficult to play and show our real ability.

As I said, self-confidence is essential for success, but it is not the only condition, because it must be based on the real ability and potential of the player. Self-confidence can never come from something else!

If you are trying to win the game with your own abilities it does not matter how confident you are in yourself and your potential. You won't be able to win with only your self-confidence. You must also have ability.

Just like motivation and stress, the connection between the level of self-confidence and the actual ability is complex.

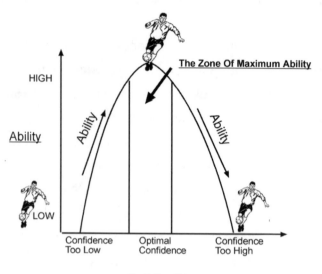

Self Confidence

The left part of the chart shows that ability grows as the level of self-confidence grows up to the point at which your level of self-confidence suits your maximum ability. Beyond this point, as your self-confidence grows your ability declines.

Pay attention, **everyone has a specific zone of maximum ability**. The idea is to know where this zone is and to regulate your level of self-confidence accordingly.

Achieving the optimal level of self-confidence and belief in ability means that you are completely certain in your ability to achieve your goals and you will invest every strength and effort to achieve them. This is not to say that you will always succeed and it does not mean you won't make mistakes. However, the belief in your ability will allow you to deal with the lack of success and your mistakes, and will guide you all the time to keep on believing and working towards your goals.

When your self-confidence in too low or too high you won't be able to express your real ability.

Low Self-confidence

Some players have talent and can be very successful, however they do not believe in their ability to succeed under pressure. These are the "training players" -there is a significant difference between their ability in practice and their ability in the real game.

Such players constantly question their ability in the game and doubts like these tend to fulfill themselves. **In other words, when your mind is dealing with doubts, you are not concentrated and you make mistakes that only strengthen your doubts and the result will be lack of self-confidence and low ability.**

In some of these cases the lack of confidence is connected only to a certain action or situation, but if the player doesn't try to alter it, the lack of confidence will influence his ability.

It is possible to work on the lack of confidence and to regulate it. **If you feel that you do not succeed in expressing your real ability and you have doubts about it, this is the time to start working on your self-confidence.**

The lack of self-confidence is not only a personal problem. In soccer, as a team game, the lack of confidence is "**contagious**". It is enough that 2 or 3 players in the team come to a game with low self-confidence and sometimes very often **the whole team** becomes full of players who play without confidence. This is one more reason why it is important that every player in the team comes to a game with **the level of self-confidence best fitting his maximum ability.**

Too High Self-confidence

Everybody remembers players with too high self-confidence. These are players that have lost the connection between their real ability and their self-confidence. We speak about players whose self-confidence is not based on talent or ability, but on false confidence. The result in such a situation is low ability on the field.

Such a player thinks that he shouldn't practice and try harder and sometimes this can lead all the players of the team to come unprepared for a game. The result in most of the cases will be a loss.

Having too much self and team confidence happens very often, when a "strong" team plays against a "weak" team (or a team that according to the press is breaking apart, is firing its coach, etc.).

In such cases, when the game starts the insufficient preparation of these players will not lead to the optimal team ability. This will only encourage and give confidence to the "weak" team and will make the situation even more difficult. This is the reason that upsets occur.

A player must come with a level of self-confidence fitting his maximum ability to every game. This is the only possible way to guarantee consistency in ability and to prevent unnecessary losses. It is compulsory to check for excess self-confidence and to regulate it to suit the level of maximum performance.

Step 13: Real self-confidence and strong belief in your abilities

Developing self-confidence and belief in ability

As with other areas related to the psychology of sport there are those who believe that self-confidence is something we are born with, but this is far from the truth.

Self-confidence **can be built**. It is true that the self-confidence of an adult is influenced by his past, but this is a process that can be changed.

Even an older player can build his self-confidence and the belief in personal ability.

Following is a list of actions you can take to strengthen your self-confidence and the belief in your ability:

<u>**Previous success**</u> strengthens self-confidence and leads you to more victories. Every soccer player must concentrate on his previous successes in order to strengthen his self-confidence. This is the place to emphasize that we are speaking about personal successes not necessarily defined as wins or championships. It is an additional proof of how important it is to define goals beyond victory and to be sure that every single player and the whole team enjoy success the whole season.

<u>Thought about previous success = Self-confidence</u>

<u>**Success in training**</u>. As a player when you perform successful actions consistently in training your self-confidence and the belief that you can perform these actions in the real game will only grow. It is important that the training sessions are as close as possible to the real game and it is also important to practice the actions you believe you can perform. It is essential to repeat again and again the successful actions.

Success in training = Self-confidence

Concentration on personal ability. In the same way that previous success strengthens your self-confidence, your previous failures can hurt your confidence. In other words, you do not have a problem with self-confidence if your team has won 5 consecutive games, but what will happen if your team loses the next 5 games? The natural reaction in such a situation is a loss of self-confidence, however this is not a law. You must teach yourself that what determines your self-confidence is not the win or the loss, but **your ability** in the game. If you did everything you were supposed to do and even though your team lost, you have no reason to doubt your ability. Your standing point should concentrate on your ability and not on the result of the last game or the last 5 games.

Be careful not to concentrate on the score. If you do so, you and the team enter a trap, because the more losses you have, so will erode the self-confidence of the players. This will lead only to additional losses and to greater damage to the self and team confidence.

In order to break this circle you must concentrate on the personal and team ability and not on the score. The right work in practice together with the belief in ability will lead to success.

Concentration on your ability, not on the result = Self-confidence

Showing assertiveness. Towards others you must always show self-confidence and belief in your ability, especially when you have taken a blow to your self-confidence or doubts are rising about your ability.

There exists a close relationship between our thoughts and feelings to our behavior. It is important that, **even if you do not feel it, you show self-confidence. Such behavior will lead eventually to higher self-confidence.**

This behavior is important for another reason as well – if you show behavior that hints about lack of confidence, belief, desperation or exhaustion you strengthen in this way your opponent (if you are a defender you strengthen the forward. If you are a forward the defender will be assured).

In every situation it is important to show behavior of self-confidence that includes:

- **Head held high**
- **Fast movement**
- **A smile**
- **Straight look in the eyes of the opponent saying, "I will beat you!"**
- **Continuing fighting, working, shouting, encouraging, etc.**
- **You make your opponent feel you are confident and you believe in your ability without any connection to the score.**

<u>**Behave as a winner = Feel like a winner =**</u>
<u>**Show Assertiveness**</u>

<u>**Positive thinking**</u>. Self-confidence is the belief and the thought that you are capable of achieving your goals. If you adopt this kind of thinking you will be able to build your self-confidence.

Be aware that compared to positive thinking, the negative thoughts only rise in you doubts about your ability to complete your goals and this hurts your self-confidence.

Positive thinking = Self-confidence

Body fitness. All the confidence in the world won't help you if you do not maintain the necessary physical fitness for achieving your goals. When you feel that you are in excellent physical condition your belief in your ability will grow as well. Physical fitness is your responsibility, not the coach's duty and not even the fitness trainer's obligation. They can assist you but the **responsibility** is only yours. Consistency in training, rest and proper nutrition will guarantee you the fitness that will allow you to achieve your real ability and will raise your self-confidence and the belief in your potential!

Physical fitness = Self-confidence

Mental preparation. The basis of your self-confidence is the full awareness that you are completely ready for the game. You cannot think, "It will be all right", if you haven't invested the necessary amount of effort before the game. If you have read the book up to now, I hope you are aware how important your mental preparation is for your success, self-confidence and the belief in your ability.

There are no shortcuts, no "It will be OK", no easy games.

Wins on paper do not give you points.

When you feel ready for the game you can also expect to win. Being ready for a game means that you have done everything possible to succeed. The right mental preparation will advance you to a state in which you know what you have to do in every situation on the field and it will give you the belief that you can succeed in everything you do. When lacking mental preparation, your self-confidence (if it exists), is lacking its deep basis that provides it with stability and consistency.

Without proper mental preparation, when things are not easy during the game, self-confidence will disappear.

Mental preparation = Self-confidence

Use of visualization. The most efficient way to work on your self-confidence, strengthen it, regulate it and preserve it for a long time is the work with visualization. In chapter 9 we used visualization to deal with stress and pressure and for mental preparation. The basis for strengthening self-confidence with the help of visualization is the imagining of your successful actions from previous games or training. Visualization will strengthen you and the belief in your abilities.

"You had good and successful actions before, you will have good and successful actions today as well"

The work with visualization for strengthening your confidence and the belief in your ability should be done every time you perform mental preparation for a game. Do this at the end of the relaxation and after you have visualized different game conditions.

Example for visualization exercise for strengthening self-confidence and the belief in ability.

- Sit down or lie with eyes closed. Imagine yourself in a successful action from your past – a good action that

gave you a lot of happiness, satisfaction and good feel
ing. Feel the image with all the senses that were involved
in it. You feel the movements you've done, you see the
ball in the net, you hear the crowd and you feel the happiness.

- Choose one steady image or one of several possible
  images. Keep the image in imagination with all the
  senses and feelings.

- Together with the image in your imagination take a deep
  breath and very slowly the image becomes more and more
  real. Tell yourself, "I feel now exactly as I felt then. I will
  feel this way in the game. I will play well in this game."

- Concentrate on the picture and let it disappear very
  slowly… still with eyes closed concentrate on your regular
  breathing and repeat with every breath, "With every breath
  of air, my self-confidence becomes greater. With every
  breath, I believe more in myself. I believe in my ability
  and I will show it in the game. I believe in my ability. I had
  good games in the past and this game too will be a good
  one."

- Remember the feeling of self-confidence you had before
  good games – games in which you succeeded in express
  ing your ability. Check how you feel right now. Try to match
  your feeling of self-confidence to the level you want. - -
  Continue working with visualization till you reach that
  optimal level…

- Count quietly in your mind from 1 to 5. With every number
  you feel that your confidence is rising and together with it
  the belief in your ability also becomes stronger. Tell yourself, "I am ready and I expect to have a good game."

- Concentrate for a minute on your breathing and slowly open your eyes...(a more detailed description of the exercise can be found at the end of the book).

In fact, the work on self-confidence doesn't end when you take the field, because during the game things happen that lower your self-confidence (not very often a situation can cause your self-confidence to rise too high and to start celebrating the victory before the final whistle. You must be careful not to enter such situations, to be aware of them and to stop them immediately). Let's suppose that in this situation you performed a couple of unsuccessful actions and you saw the coach and the other players shout at you. As a result, negative thoughts start to rise in your head and your self-confidence lowers. To prevent this from happening, you must be aware of your thoughts, you must learn to think positively and to talk to yourself only in a positive way.

In such situations you must learn to concentrate only on the action you are performing in the moment, without any connection to your previous actions.

When you feel the doubts about your ability start to rise and the belief in your ability is becoming weaker, find an opportunity (a ball out of bounds, an injury to a player, etc.) to take a deep breath and return to the same image of a successful action from your previous games.

Use the pause in the game to return to what you felt when you performed this successful action and tell yourself, "I succeeded then, I will succeed today too". Take another deep breath, tell yourself a couple of encouraging words and come back to the game. Every exercise can take you half a minute or a minute with eyes open.

If you do not have even this time, settle for a deep breath and some encouragement.

Work with visualization = Self-confidence

Self-confidence and stress

One of the major reasons for stress is the feeling of **uncertainty** that is caused by not knowing in advance what the score will be or how you will perform. It is true that you can't know the score before the game, but do you really have doubts about your ability?

When you are sure in your success and you have real self-confidence based on your ability and preparation, you do not have doubts about your ability in the game. You are sure you will succeed in showing your maximum ability and your level of stress will be low. In situations like that you have no reason to be tense.

Level of stress matching your maximum ability = Self-confidence

A player with a full belief in his ability and with real self-confidence will not feel tense!!! You are under pressure only when you have doubts about your ability in the game.

Summary

- Self-confidence, emotional control and concentration are important for your success and you must work on them.
- Self-confidence can be acquired and regulated. You can develop self-confidence with training.

- Learn from your previous games what your optimal level of self-confidence is and always take the field with it.
- Belief in ability = Self-confidence
- Positive thinking = Self-confidence
- Physical fitness = Self-confidence
- Mental preparation = Self-confidence
- Visualization = Self-confidence
- Behaving assertively = Self-confidence
- Concentrating on your ability and not on the score = Self-confidence
- Level of stress matching your maximum ability = Self-confidence and belief in ability

The Coach Box

Self-confidence and belief in ability are personal qualities that every player should have. However, you as a coach have direct influence on these qualities and with them on the player's ability on the field.

Tell each of your players that you have expectations from him and you **deeply believe** that he is capable of standing up to them. Your expectations should be, of course, realistic.

Keep showing to every player that you continue to believe in him, without any connection to his ability on the field in a specific game, and see how much effort he invests in order to see that you are right. Your belief in his ability strengthens his own belief in his ability and from here the road to better ability is closer. Of course, it doesn't always work this way and sometimes you have no choice but to take the player out of the starting line-up. However, even then, don't transmit that you have lost hope with him or that he is a failure. **It is true that his ability is low, but you still believe in him and you convince him that if he works hard... etc**.

Beyond showing your belief in the players and the team, the feedback they receive from you is also very important. **Learn to be always positive even when you try to correct mistakes. Always start with a positive word and after it give your remark about the mistakes and at the end say another positive word.**

With time you will see how this behavior makes miracles. Example: **"You gave a very good effort, next time, pass to the left forward, lets win the game ...!"**

You as a coach, must show assertive behavior all the time and belief in your own and your team's ability.

Chapter 18 – Emotional Control

Step 14: Emotional control means – to play soccer only with your head and feet, without emotions

Emotional control is one of the elements of mental strength. Emotional control, as its name says, is our ability to control emotions. It is a very important key for successful expression of our real ability.

You cannot be a high level athlete in any kind of sport without emotional control!

In the eastern marshal arts the fighters train to achieve full control over their emotions – until they reach a state of calmness that allows them to control their emotions even in extremely stressful situations. We do not plan, indeed, to reach such a level of emotional control, but the more we control our emotions, the better able we will be to show our full ability.

What happens when a player does not control his emotions?

Exaggerated Aggressiveness and Violence find expression in hard fouls that eventually lead to the sending off of the player.

Low reaction threshold makes the player lash out at his teammates, the referee etc.

Impulsiveness – reaction without thinking or control (a player fouls me – retaliate and the result is a yellow card at least or even a sending off).

The anger at the coach / opponent / teammate or at yourself hurts your ability to concentrate,

your decision making abilities
and ultimately your performance.

When you kick the ball with anger, the chances that it will reach the place you wanted are meager.

Lack of emotional control can express itself in many more emotions that influence you. For example, extreme happiness that hurts your concentration, depression that lowers your confidence- and disappointment that leads to excessive violence.

Fear and anxiety, like any other feeling that is not under your full emotional control, hurt your ability to concentrate, your self-confidence and of course your ability.

I already wrote that soccer players are only human and the appearance of emotions during the game is a normal reaction. The idea is not to terminate your feelings (this is possible only in robots). We are trying to achieve control over our emotions, which means being aware of the feeling and its intensity when it rises inside us, to control it and to react as much as possible without the influence of the emotions.

In the eastern arts of war the goal is to bring the mind to a state in which it is calm and peaceful like a clear pool of water and everything reflecting in it. Actually, the feelings influence our mind the same way the wind or a rock disturb the image in the pool of water and distort its contours.

Feelings disturb your perception and concentration and do not allow you to achieve your maximum potential.

Your emotional control should be expressed when you kick or head the ball. You should perform the header with your

head alone and the kick only with your foot, without the influence of your feelings. You should not kick with anger, disappointment, fear or joy. Your kick should be done only with the foot or only with the head when you are heading (enough goals are missed from situations that "are impossible" to miss, because the kicker began to celebrate the goal he scored, before he kicked the ball). Beyond the particular kick or header, every movement and your behavior on the field should be done with full emotional control. This does not mean you do not experience feelings, **you feel but you are in control.**

It is important to remember that the influence of the feelings is always negative, even when it is a positive feeling like joy.

When a team scores a goal and its players do not succeed in controlling their joy, if they are not concentrated on the restart of the game they might very often give up a goal.

What can be done?

Stress control. One of the major reasons for the appearance of negative emotions during the game is stress. We already said that stress raises feelings of fear, anxiety and aggressiveness and at the same time it also lowers our reaction threshold. This combination is a very serious problem. The rise of aggressiveness combined with a lower reaction threshold might cause us to react with exaggerated violence to the remark of a friend, a foul by an opponent or the referee's judgment.

You must cope with stress because of many reasons, but the main one is the need to control your emotions. This will help you to enter the game with the stress level best fitting your maximum ability.

Emotional awareness. Pay attention to what is happening with your emotions during the game. Learn to distinguish between them and to name them. Tell yourself that now joy or anger or any other feeling overwhelms you. When you define your feelings with the right names, try to regulate their intensity. Try to put the feelings aside and to concentrate on the game.

Use self-talk. Regulating your emotions can be done with efficient self-talk. You can do this if you say to yourself sentences like:

"I enjoyed it enough, I will continue after the final whistle."

"The real joy will be in the changing room."

"Good ability and emotions don't go together."

"Anger only disturbs me, I will concentrate on the game."

"When I am angry – I help the opponent."

"My revenge is to play better."

Use key words. As a part of your self-talk you can use key words to prevent yourself from dealing with the emotions. Simply adopt the word **"STOP!"** and every time you notice your feelings are rising, say **"STOP!"** to yourself. You can do this aloud or silently, and together with it you must stop dealing with your feelings and regain the emotional control.

Impulsive reaction – impulsive reaction is an instinctive reaction that is done without thinking and taking into account its consequences. For example, you have been kicked and you immediately retaliate. The referee decided against you and you start yelling at him. A player curses you and you curse him back.

You understand, of course, that impulsive reactions and sport do not go together. The impulsive reaction is an expression of a lack of emotional control and it will lead to a yellow card or a red and out of the game.

If you want to be a good player, you must avoid acting impulsively on the field. It is much easier said than done. We are all only human and some of our reactions are impulsive.

When dealing with sport we must change the impulsive reactions. You can do this simply by starting to habituate yourself every time you want to react immediately in practice or in the game to first take a deep breath and to concentrate on it instead on your feelings. It is difficult, but possible. Of course, it takes practice and you can use the team practice in which you also have enough chances where you want to react impulsively. In situations like these learn to act differently. Take a deep breath concentrate on it and react only then. If it is hard for you to take the deep breath use key words: "STOP!" or any other word you choose, before you react.

Another good way to reestablish emotional control is working on emotional control with visualization. As a part of your mental preparation for the game, work with visualization on the game situations, in which you behave impulsively (a hard foul against you, an opponent cursing, pinching or spitting at you, etc.) Imagine these situations and see yourself react with full control, giving the proper sportsman like reaction or ignoring it.

Your control should be not only towards others, but also towards yourself. It is important not to react with anger, but it is just as important not to gather the anger inside of you, because eventually the anger will find its expression.

With visualization, teach yourself simply not to react, not in your behavior and not with your feelings.

Depression

Players, like everyone else, tend sometimes to enter a state of depression that expresses itself on the field in a lack of desire to play, lack of enthusiasm, indifference, lack of power, heavy movement and low level of energy. It is very difficult to have a good game when you are in a state like that.

The problem in such situations is that the depression hurts your ability and as a result the feeling of depression becomes stronger. This leads the player into a magic circle that is very hard to break through. If the player's feeling of depression is not altered immediately it can hurt his ability for a long period of time. **Of course, that decline in ability will cause the removal of the player from the line-up, which will only strengthen the feeling of depression and helplessness.**

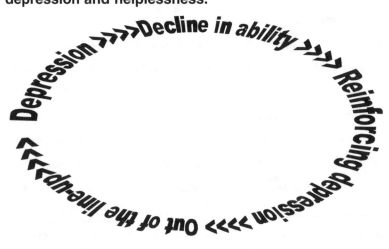

We all believe that we can succeed in overcoming depression with our own powers and return to our regular selves. The reality is not always the same. A player must be aware of his emotional condition and if the feeling of depression does not leave him after a week or two, it is time to call a psychologist.

This treatment is right not only for you. You must be aware of what is happening to the other players in the team and if you suspect that one of the players is in trouble, don't hesitate to talk with the coaching staff.

A different topic that is connected to the emotional state of athletes is "**eating disorders**". In recent years there have been cases in both young, and professional soccer players who suffered form eating disorders. Speaking in professional terms these are **anorexia and bulimia**. The outside expression of these disorders is the extreme weight loss or exaggerated eating without gaining weight. **If these disorders are not treated they might lead to the end of the player's career and even to death.**

I want to emphasize again the importance of being aware of what is happening to you and the rest of the players in your team. If it seems to you that you or another player has a problem you must look for professional help.

Just as when your leg hurts for a week or two and you go to a physiotherapist or a doctor without hesitation, you must also treat your emotional problem and speak with a psychologist. The result of the lack of treatment in both cases is identical – a decline in your ability with everything that follows from that. It is not a shame and not a weakness and there is no significant difference between calling an orthopedist or a psychologist.

Detachment

Soccer players live and work in the real world outside of their team or sport. As people, we experience things that produce positive or negative feelings: breaking up with a girlfriend the night before the game, house quarrels, your child or a relative is sick, your girlfriend agreed to marry you, you became a father etc. All these events make us feel different feelings (positive or negative).

The problem arises because such feelings are incompatible with a game or training. **A player must learn to isolate these feelings during the game. It is not simple, but it is possible**. The starting point is:

Be aware of your emotions and don't deny them.

In your mental preparation for the game, work on yourself and try to put the feelings aside. They will wait for you after the game.

You cannot take the field with the feelings you bring.
They will hurt your game.

In the following chapter we deal with concentration and there also we will speak about the necessity for detachment.

Feelings and sensations of maximum performance

Our goal is to be in an emotional state fitted to our maximum ability. To be self-confident and with belief in ability. To have emotional control and security and the belief that all we start will succeed.

Every player has such games and you too had games in which you felt you succeeded in expressing your real ability. **Learn to return to these games in your imagination and try to copy from them the feeling you had before and during the game.**

Your goal: to be in the emotional state fitting your maximum ability before and throughout the game.

If you advance and come closer to this state you will become a better and more consistent player – a stable player that can be trusted. This is the player who is liked and respected by coaches and teammates.

Summary

- Emotional control is essential for success in sport.
- In order to control your feelings you must be aware of them and their intensity.
- Your goal is to regulate your emotions to a level fitting your maximum ability.
- You kick the ball only with your foot, not with your feelings and you are heading only with your head.
- It is necessary to control and regulate positive feelings such as joy.
- Controlling and regulating stress is essential for control and regulation of emotions.
- You can regulate emotions with positive self-talk.
- You must use key words for emotional control.
- Impulsive reactions bring you only the red card.
- Training is the place to start practicing regulation and control of your emotions.
- Depression and eating disorders endanger a players' career. Be aware of their existence.
- Calling a psychologist is identical to calling an orthopedist. In both cases – if you have a problem, you must look for professional assistance.
- Isolating the emotions that are not a part of the game is essential for your success.

The Coach Box

Emotional control is not only necessary for the players' success; it is essential for your success as a coach. You should also learn to control and regulate your emotions. If you succeed in this you will not only strengthen your health, but you will function more efficiently as a coach as well.

As a coach, you must achieve a state in which your decisions are not influenced by your feelings, but only by your professional analysis. When you are flooded by emotions (anger, joy, disappointment or all of them together) learn not to react – not to your players and not to the press. Take a couple of deep breaths, calm down, and reach control over your emotions and only then you can react.

The last thing a player needs in the heat of the game and the feelings that threaten to overwhelm him, is a coach who doesn't control his emotions.

Beyond that you won't be able to require emotional control from your players if you are not **a good example** for them! Practice what you preach!

A coach who runs wild on the field doesn't help his players!

As I already said, training is the place where practice on emotional control and regulation should begin. Your duty as a coach is to talk about it with your players and to require them to work on their emotions.

If you want to avoid yellow and red cards, you must not accept impulsive behavior during training. You can do this with practicing on special game situations that spring powerful feelings that might get out of control or hurt concentration. (Situations like giving up a goal, after scoring, being hit by a player, a serious injury of a fellow player, sending off a player, etc.) We will talk about these situations later in the book.

Chapter 19 – Concentration

Concentration is the most important element of mental strength. Concentration is not only the most important element of mental strength it is also the most sensitive element. The problem is that any action, even the simplest one, requires concentration.

Even when it seems to you that you are kicking the ball automatically, it still involves a certain amount of concentration. If you want the ball to go where you want on every kick, pass or header your head or foot must reach the right place at the right time, with the correct speed and angle. All these require **concentration**. The smallest displacement of any one of them sends the ball in the wrong direction and it won't reach its destination.

Lack of concentration is your worst enemy!

The need to be concentrated for 90 minutes, starting with the opening whistle and ending with the closing one, is the biggest difficulty for the professional player. He has no time outs, no option to go out and to come back later, no chance to rest. This fact makes soccer one of the most difficult ball games (in all the other games, players can be changed without any restrictions and there are time outs).

One second without concentration- might be the difference between winning and losing.

Keeping concentration for a long time requires investing effort and because of that it's exhausting. Look at your goalkeeper at the end of a game. Though he seemingly didn't exert himself very much, notice how exhausted he is physically and mentally. The only reason for this is the effort he invests to stay concentrated all the time.

I mentioned earlier that the elements of mental strength are influenced and influence each other and this is most salient in concentration. Lack of concentration hurts self-confidence, but lack of self-confidence hurts concentration as well. The same with emotional control: when you don't have it, concentration suffers and lack of concentration hurts emotional control. Beyond that concentration is impaired as a result of stress.

I said in the earlier chapters that one of the characteristics of stress is that it impairs concentration. When you are under pressure you certainly cannot be concentrated – you do not control your thoughts and you are busy with the different stimuli occupying your mind – the roar of the crowd, the TV cameras, the weather, the lights, the shouting of the coach and the players, etc.

In this chapter we will try to understand what concentration is, how we can strengthen it and what distracts us.

A good definition for concentration has two elements:
- Paying attention to relevant information and ignoring irrelevant and disturbing stimuli.
- Paying attention for a long period of time.

What is relevant information?

Let's take for example a situation in which the player is about to kick a penalty, two minutes before the end of the game and the score is 0 : 0. The relevant information in this situation is:

- The goal
- The position and the movements of the goalkeeper
- The position of the ball and the movement of the body and the feet when kicking the ball.

What is irrelevant /disturbing information in such a situation?

- The roar of the crowd
- The photographers next to the goal
- The other players.
- The things they say to you.
- The crowd behind the goal.
- The TV guy with the camera behind the net.
- Thoughts like, "What if I miss?", "This goalkeeper saves a lot of penalties", "We won the game", "This is the most important kick in my career" and many more.

If the player wants to kick the ball successfully he must concentrate on the relevant information and ignore all the other disturbing factors – external and internal.

The second element from the definition is dealing with time. We must keep **the same amount of attention** for the whole 90 minutes. It is relatively easy to disregard irrelevant information when performing a certain kick, it is very difficult to keep concentration from the opening whistle until the end of the game.

Part of this difficulty results from the fact that there isn't only one type of concentration but several types, and throughout the game we must change swiftly between one type of concentration to another.

Let's continue with the example of the penalty kick. The

concentration needed for performing the kick is **narrow and defined**. I mean that the player in this situation must process information from a narrow area within his visual field. Even if his eyes see everything (the goalkeeper, the goal , the crowd, the stadium, the sky, etc.) the player must concentrate only on what is happening between him, the ball and the goal.

Narrow concentration is not suitable to other situations in the game. For example, when a player is moving with the ball he must decide what to do with it. His concentration certainly should be on the ball (narrow concentration), but he should also see the extended image of the whole field with the position of the other players from the team, the position of the opponents and so on. This second type of concentration is called **broad concentration**. A good player must be capable of switching between the two types of concentration according to the game conditions.

Not all players have the same concentration abilities. Some players see the game and are good at kicking the ball 30 meters between two opponents to a teammate. This ability requires broad concentration. On the other hand, the penalty kicker of the team should be a player who can keep narrow concentration when kicking the ball.

As a player you must be capable of matching the types of concentration to the situations in the game and to your role. Too much emphasis on one of the types of concentration will lead to mistakes and to lost opportunities. For example, if you have only narrow concentration, like guarding a player without paying attention to what is happening around you (the position of teammates and the opposing players), even if you succeed in neutralizing the player you guard, there might be situations in which you won't be aware that your help was needed to cover a teammate or you won't see an open player to pass him the ball, because the transition from narrow to broad concentration will be too slow.

What disturbs our concentration?
We already mentioned some of the things
in the earlier chapters of this book.
In fact almost everything we spoke about up to now
influences your concentration as well:

<u>**Concentrating on the past and not on the present**</u>. For example, when we are stuck with an action that was already done, when we are angry at someone's mistake or when we are flooded with joy after a successful action. Take for example, close to the end of the game with the score 1:0 ,a forward from the team that leads needs to guard a forward from the other team, on a free kick. He does not guard him well and as a result the forward scores and ties the game. In this moment all the players from the team start yelling at their forward and blame him for the goal. Right after the restart of the game, this forward is in a clear position to score, but his kick goes awkwardly outside. The player is still under the influence of the reactions of the other players about the goal they allowed. He is concentrated on the past instead of concentrating on the present and he does not succeed.

<u>**Concentrating on the future and not on the present**</u>. When your thoughts wanderthings such as the consequences of the game, you impair your concentration again. In cases like this, instead of concentrating on the field, you concentrate on thoughts like, "What if we lose", "What if I get an injury", "How do I celebrate the win", "What will I do with the win bonus" etc.

Sometimes you can see a player who is in a situation where he can't miss and even then he fails to score. The reason, in many cases, is concentration on the future instead of on the present. The player begins to celebrate the goal before he has scored it and because of this concentration on the future he misses.

Paying attention to too many details. A player who's concentration is too broad might lose his concentration, because his attention is placed on things outside the field – the audience, the photographers, the lights, the weather, the curses of the crowd and more. When a player is stuck in a state of too broad concentration he might make mistakes in even the simplest actions.

The crowd, of course, can influence every player. Even in games when there is a small crowd, the players hear the curses of the crowd and are more influenced by them in comparison to games when the crowd is large and the curses disappear in the general turmoil. Anyway, **when you are concentrated on the crowd, you are not fully in the game** and your concentration is too broad.

Over-concentration on the body. A player who is concentrated on what is happening to his body is not concentrated on what is happening on the field. When our concentration is busy with our aches and pains we won't be capable of showing our maximum ability, because in such situations our concentration becomes narrow and internally focused. It is dealing with details not connected to the game.

Time after time the press glorifies an injured player who continues to play and "sacrifices" himself for the team. However, is it really a situation to praise and do coaches have to agree with it?

A player who plays with an injury in addition to the fact that he endangers himself and can worsen the injury (and be missing for a long time) usually won't be able at all to concentrate on what is happening on the field, because he can't ignore the pain. Such a player must make mistakes!!! It is true that you can require a professional player to play well even when it hurts him (on the condition that it does not endanger his health) and on the condition that the coach knows the player and is certain that he can do this. However, we are all human and only few of us are not influenced by pain.

For example, in the National League Championship a team had a 3:2 lead about 5 minutes before the end of the game. The team's goalkeeper got injured. The substitute goalkeeper was already warmed up because of a previous injury of the goalkeeper in this game and was able to replace him immediately. However, the injured goalkeeper did not agree to go out and continued playing while everyone saw him suffer. In the 90th minute the referee gives a free kick against his team from a reasonable distance. When the ball is kicked towards the goal the goalkeeper is late in his reaction and gives up a goal. It is clear that if the goalkeeper was concentrated on the free kick instead of on his body he would have stopped the ball. This is the reason that you as a player and coach must be aware of your physical condition. If you see that your attention is directed towards your pain and you are not concentrated on the game, as a professional – it is best for you and for the team to ask to be substituted.

Stress. We dealt with stress in the previous chapters and if you are still not convinced that stress prevents you from demonstrating your maximum ability, maybe you will be persuaded by its damaging effect on your concentration.

Stress impairs concentration!

Actually, the mere definition of stress is related to loss of concentration. When you are tense, you are not able to read this book (it's true that you leaf through the book, but you have no idea what you read) or not even concentrate on the TV (you are looking at the "box", but you don't know exactly what is going on in the movie). **So how would you succeed in situations like these to be a good player?**

The pressure prevents you from concentrating on the relevant information for your success as a player and makes you concentrate on the contrary on the details that disturb you – like thoughts, feelings, anxiety, surplus of information and more.

In order to be able to demonstrate your full potential starting from the first minute of the game, you have to enter the field with a stress level matching your maximum ability. Every deviation in the level of stress will impair your concentration and your play.

Exhaustion. Fatigue is also a factor that hurts concentration. When you are tired, naturally you concentrate on your body and again the concentration is impaired. We already said that keeping concentration for a long time is very exhausting and when you are tired you have less resources to keep your concentration. This is the place to remind you of the importance of physical fitness for maintaining concentration.

What do we do to preserve concentration for a long period of time?

Let's start with an example of a team in its best concentration state. In a national league game several spectators were hurt by the collapse of a set of bleachers. In order to evacuate the wounded an ambulance enters the side of the field driving in the direction of the accident. The game is not stopped and the players continue to play. The result was 1 : 0 for the home team. With just minutes before the end of the game, the guest team was pressing to equal the score. In the analysis I performed I found that most of the home team players neither heard the collapse nor saw the ambulance driving around the field.

They succeeded in limiting their concentration exactly to the right range and as a result they managed to ignore the information that was irrelevant for their success on the field.

How do we do this?

On the one hand, you should learn to know yourself. Check if you tend to place your attention narrowly or broadly and if you have difficulty with one of these kinds of concentration. Check if you can switch easily between narrow to broad concentration or if you have difficulty with it. Check if you can be concentrated for 90 minutes or that in the first 5 minutes and in the minutes at the end of the game you are less concentrated. Check with yourself if a large audience makes you lose your concentration. In the same way, discover if an important game, a televised game, the presence of the national team coach or a representative of a foreign team influence your attention.

Answer sincerely, because only if you know what impairs your concentration and when, will you be able to work with yourself and improve your concentration ability.

After you have managed to recognize the difficulties you experience with your concentration and with keeping it for a long time, check with yourself if it is possible that the factors leading to loss of concentration are related to your body. In other words, if you have an injury and you don't treat it, because you don't want to lose your place in the line-up or if you have pain during the game.

If it is not an injury that impairs your concentration, check if it might be a problem with your physical preparation. Think again sincerely with yourself and check if you have the fitness to play with the same tempo throughout the game. See if in the last minutes of the game you run out of power.

In case you are certain that your fitness is not a problem you can conclude from this that **your concentration is impaired, because of mental reasons and this can be changed with the right work.**

<u>**Control your thoughts and emotions**</u> (we spoke about it in the previous chapters). Learn to immediately recognize the situations in which irrelevant thoughts enter your mind – thoughts about the past or the future, and stop them right away. To stop these thoughts from appearing you should train to stop them. As I said, this is a simple technique: the moment you recognize the beginning of a thought command yourself, "Stop!". You can also follow the order with the execution of a body action or a series of actions like clapping hands, fisting or waving your hand, a deep

breath or any other movement suitable to you. Turn this into a habit. Start working on it in your regular training. After you practice it enough, you will see that this simple exercise works in the game as good as in training. The best proof that you have learned this skill will be that with time you will notice you are using the exercise less and less. In other words, the frequency of the thoughts will decline.

Learn to recognize and regulate every emotion and every thought that occupy you according to the instructions of the previous chapter.

Turn every negative thought into positive (we dealt with this topic in previous chapters). It is preferable, of course, that you do not have negative thoughts. However, if they appear change them into positive.

Control the eyes.

Literally it can be said that your concentration is where your eyes are.

When your look gets out of the confines of the field in the direction of the stadium, the crowd, etc. your concentration also is directed with it. Learn to control your eyes. Keep them inside the limits of the field in any case, without taking into account what is happening out of it. Your eyes should be on the field. As a soccer player, you mostly depend on the information you receive from your vision. When your vision field is too wide or fixed outside the field the information important for your success as a player won't be able to reach you – the position of the ball, the players, etc. With the situation on the field changing all the time you cannot relax your eyes. Letting them rest is leaving aside your concentration.

Use key words. Write down several suitable words you can use during the game as a hint to change your behavior or style of play. In the same way we used the word "stop", to block our thoughts, we can use key words to control and regulate the emotions resulting from these thoughts. We can use key words like – **concentrate, come on, be bad, attack, I did it**, etc. When in the game, if you feel a decline in your concentration or in your ability, shout in your mind a couple of times the key word you have chosen and in the following minutes change your game style to be more intensive and aggressive (however, don't lose emotional control. Don't run wild!). If your concentration is narrow and only on the ball or on the player with it, expand it very slowly to the whole field and return to showing your full ability. **You can choose any word in any language you want, this is your secret. What is important is that you are aware of your concentration and when there is a need you can use the word you have chosen to change your play style accordingly. Start using key words in training and notice how it improves your game**.

Learn not to evaluate your actions while you are playing. One of the reasons for loss of concentration is when you begin to give yourself marks for the actions you take (good or bad). In this way, you judge yourself. In soccer there is no player who succeeds in every action, pass or kick he makes. However, from the moment you start to judge yourself you reach generalizations like, "It is not my day", "I can't score with this goalkeeper", "I can't make a pass today" etc. It is true that you must be aware of your actions and their consequences, but you cannot criticize yourself. If you missed a ball tell yourself the truth ("I didn't place my foot/body in the right way / I wasn't concentrated / In a situation like that it is better to pass the ball" etc.) and continue playing without evaluating yourself. In this way at the next opportunity you will perform the right actions and won't miss this time. Take in account that when you criticize yourself you lose your concentration.

When you are busy "criticizing yourself" your play will get worse and you might get once again into a magic circle.

Start practicing this way thinking in your training
and later in the real games too.

<u>**Try training in the presence of disturbing factors**</u>. It is true that this is not always possible, because if a large crowd takes you out of concentration it will be difficult to gather such a crowd in your training (in some cases you can use loudspeakers to create the experience of a large and noisy crowd). Anyway, there are enough factors disturbing your concentration that can be simulated during practice. For example, if the weather disturbs your attention this is a pretty good reason to practice also in harsh weather conditions if they are expected during the game. **As a rule, it is important to train in conditions as similar as possible to the conditions during the real game.** If a bad field hurts your concentration or demands a higher level of concentration from you and you know that the game will be played on such a field, try practicing several times on a similar field. It is essential to train in the presence of the factors disturbing you (as much as possible), **although our natural tendency is to train the things we are good at and in the conditions comfortable to us.** This is why a player whose right

leg is stronger prefers to kick with it in training instead of using the practice to strengthen his weaker leg. In the same way there are only a few players who love to practice in rain / strong wind / extreme heat. It is much more comfortable to cancel training because of the weather conditions or to move it indoors (and certainly it is good to do so from time to time). However, such practice won't help your ability during the game if you will have to play in the same harsh weather conditions. This is also relevant about practicing without leg protectors, etc.

Establish a regular set of actions – a ritual. The intention is about the performance of a certain set of actions every time your concentration is hurt and you do not succeed in concentrating on the game or when the game is about to begin and the stress and pressure cause you to lose your concentration. You can achieve this with the performance of actions like regular stretching, walking, juggling (not during the game), certain words together with clenching your fist, clapping hands, etc. I speak about simple actions that you can perform also in the game, when there is a break of a few seconds. When you perform the line of actions or a specific act you concentrate only on their completion. Your concentration on these actions will help you prevent your attention from running away into disturbing factors   (several NBA players say a few words to themselves, twist or bounce the ball before free throws). It is true that this can be explained as superstition, but because it helps concentration it doesn't matter how it is explained.

Superstition. In my opinion, there is nothing bad in superstition if it does not impair your self-confidence and concentration as long as you control the things you believe in. If you believe that putting your right shoe before the left one is a remedy for success, there is no reason not to believe in that. However if you have only one pair of "winning" socks, this might be a problem, because there will be situations in which you won't be able to play with them. It is important to choose the beliefs that **help you and are under your control**. For example, the way you put your shoes on or tie them up, entering the changing room or the field with the right leg, kicking the wall before the game, a short prayer, laughing together before entering the field or any other thing that can always be done. **It is not recommended to use superstitions connected to the color of your clothes, a specific pair of socks or underwear, the side you attack in the first half etc. When relying on superstition it is important to allow some kind of choice. In this way if one of the actions cannot be done, it will be possible to use the good influence of the other beliefs**. The most important thing when using superstition is self-confidence and concentration. If the existence of superstition helps them it is for a good cause.

<u>**Practice neutralizing the influence of a large noisy crowd**</u>. Some of the players are influenced by the presence of a big and especially unfriendly audience. Players have difficulty focusing their attention and preserving the concentration in such games. **Our ears and eyes find it hard to remain inside the field and run away to the stadium. And our concentration follows the eyes**. Usually the weakening of the concentration happens in the first minutes of the game. The following exercise will help you ignore the crowd in such situations and concentrate on yourself:
- When you enter the field for a warm-up, stand up and look at the crowd, but instead of concentrating on the people concentrate on the colors.

- Chose several colors and look for them first in the last rows of the stadium then very slowly start lowering your look still concentrating on the colors.
- Continue lowering your look to the bottom row. Then follow the colors around the field.
- From there, look at the color of the grass, then very slowly look at the color of your shoes.
- Look now at your socks, the color of your pants and your shirt. You are now concentrated and the crowd does not disturb you.
- Concentrate on the color of your shirt. Take a deep breath and tell yourself while exhaling that together with it you are blowing away everything that impairs your concentration. You are going to play your best!!!
- If necessary repeat again.
- Now you are ready to start warming up.

Deal with difficulties concentrating before an important game. There will be times that whatever you do it is still difficult for you to concentrate. For example, when you are about to participate in an especially important game for you. In such situations, when you take the field and you are not concentrated, warm up more intensely than usual. It is important to feel your muscles in the warm-up. Start concentrating on your body and muscles. Try to attend only to the feeling of your body. Clear your mind from any thoughts and be aware only of your body. Continue with the warm-up in the same way until you enter the field before the game begins. Then widen your concentration and focus your attention on the players and the field instead. If you still have not reached full concentration, match your game style in the beginning of the game to your concentration. On the one hand invest physical effort, on the other try to perform simple actions, sure passes and not passing the ball 30 meters between 5 opposing players. Pass the ball instead of keeping it and trying to go through a defender. In this way you can gradually build your concentration and return to your regular level of play.

Detachment. In order to be concentrated on the game you must learn to disengage from everything that is not related to the game. This does not mean to forget only about what is happening around the field. You should also put aside what happened earlier at home, what you read in the paper or heard on the radio, your thoughts and emotions. You should learn to leave aside everything that is not relevant for the game. As we already know, we are only human and it is not simple, but it is absolutely possible.

I mean not only to disengage from the things that happened before the game, but also from the things that will happen. You should learn to put aside all the irrelevant information, like the curses of the crowd, the cameras, etc. You can achieve this mainly with the right mental preparation and with the right attitude to the factors mentioned earlier (emotional control, control over your thoughts, self-talk, key words, etc.)

Play only in the present. Actually, the intention is to keep your attention on the present and what is happening at that moment in the game. It is essential for achieving your maximum ability. Take into account that naturally your mind processes information about the past and the future and it will be difficult to remain focused on the present. Your mind wants to repeat the kick or your last action and it is also busy calculating the consequences of a win or a loss in the game.

> **If you allow your mind to deal with the past or the future, your ability at present will be far away from your real ability.**

To remain concentrated on the present throughout the game requires a lot of effort. That's why you must learn first to be aware of the direction of your attention (present, past or future) and to use the suitable key-words that can return your concentration swiftly back to the present. **When your thought is not on the field, your concentration and actually you aren't there either**. To remain fully concentrated, the body and the mind should be **in the same time at the same place**. When your thoughts are wandering in the past or the future and your body is still in the present there is a **disharmony** between your place on the field in the present and your mind, which is dealing with the past or the future. This hurts your concentration, makes you commit mistakes and prevents you from showing your maximum ability. Your thoughts must be focused on the place you are - on the field, the present, the movements you perform in this moment and the ball that is approaching you. If you **always** keep the match between your place on the field and your mind you can be a better player. It is important to remember that it is not enough to be concentrated on the present before each game. Your concentration should remain there **throughout the whole game**.

> **Be always watchful and don't let your thoughts take you back or forward.**

Be in place. The place goes together with time. **You should be here and now**. Where is here? Here is the game on the field, here are your duties in the game, here is following the instructions the coach gave you, here is to be together with your team. It may sound simple, but let's check the following examples: Ron is a prominent forward in his team. He loses a ball in attack against a defender. He is sure there was a foul against him, however the referee didn't blow the whistle. Ron is angry, complains to the referee and continues with the game, however his mind is dealing with the referee. After a few minutes the referee decides on an offside against him and again he is sure this was another wrong decision and his anger grows. From this moment Ron begins to attend to the referee's judgments with the recurring thought "The referee hates my team. He always judges against us." Several minutes have passed and Ron has the perfect opportunity to score, but he misses. This example illustrates that Ron concentrated on the present but not on the right place. Instead of being a forward he became a judge of the referee. As a result his concentration and ability ware impaired. As a player you should always be "**here**". You are not a judge and not a coach ("If I were the coach I would have already replaced..." and similar thoughts). "**Here**" means that your mind is concentrated entirely on the field. You are not occupied by your girlfriend in the stadium, by the approaching holiday, with how nice it will be in the Jacuzzi after the game, with the next trip of the national team, with the possibility that next season you might be playing somewhere else, with what the coach will say in the changing room or with any other thought that takes you away from your place.

**To show your maximum ability,
you should be here and now the whole game.**

Always prepare mentally. In fact, **the solution for most of the problems that are related to preserving concentration is a good mental preparation**, as described in the previous chapters.

When you are mentally ready for the game, your concentration is also in the right place and time. Because of that, you should prepare with visualization for the game and work on your concentration as well. When you are concentrating on your preparation for executing your personal and team duty in the game you know that your concentration is the key to success. Pay attention, working with visualization, as a part of the game preparation will improve your concentration (look at exercise 3).

Is it possible to work and train to improve concentration?
The answer is **Yes!**

How can you do that?
The first stage, when training to improve your concentration, is the awareness about the factors disturbing your concentration. In this chapter you read about different problems that may prevent you from keeping your concentration and I offer you some possible solutions.

In the next stage, your training is based on your experience. After you have found what makes you lose concentration, you should fix it, change it and take advantage of what I offer you. Learn to exploit training for working on your concentration. This is the exact time and place to start your training. Improving your concentration in practice will lead you to deeper concentration in your game.

At the end of the chapter, I offer several simple exercises that will help you improve your concentration abilities. The exercises should be performed at home. They can teach you about the difficulties you experience when preserving your concentration for long periods of time and about the effort you invest to change your concentration from narrow to broad.

Exercise 1

Read the instructions through and then start with the exercise.

- Sit in front of the window / the balcony in your house and look at the surroundings you can see and hear. Try to see an image as broad as possible. Keep your concentration on this broad view for about 2 minutes. Choose a small element from the picture (a tree, a parked car, a flower or anything else) and try to concentrate only on it. Pay atten tion to all the details (color, movement, texture, etc.). Concentrate now on this object for about 2 minutes.
- Concentrate back on the broad image. Try to see an image as broad as possible and concentrate on it for about 2 more minutes. Then, concentrate back on the single object for another 2 minutes.

Check with yourself now if you succeeded keeping broad concentration. Did you manage to transfer easily from focused concentration and did you succeed in keeping focused concentration? Did you succeed in transferring easily to focused concentration and did you manage to keep it? Check if you managed to transfer from focused to broad concentration. What disturbed you and diverted your attention? What kind of thoughts arose in you.

Be aware of what disturbs you and continue performing this exercise until you manage to complete it without any disturbance. After you have finished the whole exercise, try to perform it for a longer time and transfer faster from broad to focused concentration.

When you are convinced that you perform the exercise with success, try it with the TV on next to you, or listening to a radio broadcast, music, etc.

Exercise 2

Read the instructions through and then start with the exercise. I'm sure that you keep a ball in your room. If not choose another object.

- Sit in your room and concentrate on the ball (or on any other object) in front of you.
- If you have a timer on your watch, work with it (if not, remember when you start the exercise). Concentrate on the ball, on its shape, color, on what is written on it, on its stitches. Keep your concentration only on the ball.
- The moment your thought runs away from the ball, stop and measure the time.

The exercise seems easy to perform, but in reality it is not so simple. Perform the exercise until you manage to keep your concentration continuously for 5 minutes (Do not cheat! If 5 minutes of concentration on the ball is a tough assignment, no doubt keeping concentration for 90 minutes is hard too!).

Now, when you are trained and you can preserve your concentration for 5 minutes, try to perform the exercise in the presence of disturbing factors like music, TV, an open window, etc.

Exercise 3

Read the instructions through and then start with the exercise.

- Sit or lie comfortably and close your eyes.
- Concentrate on your breathing.
- Imagine yourself in the next game. It happens to you in this very moment. The ball is with an opposing player next to you. Concentrate only on the ball. The movement of the

player doesn't bother you. You are concentrated only on the ball. Your concentration on the ball allows you to go for the ball and to take it. See yourself heading for the ball with determination and confidence. You take the ball. Concentrate now on the broad image. See the position of your teammates and how they move. Look at the position of the opponents and see yourself make an exact pass.

- Return again and again to such images in different situations on the field (attack or defense), at different places and with different decisions (a close or a long pass, kick at the goal, etc.)

Work with visualization for 2 – 3 minutes every time. In other words, you visualize for 2 – 3 minutes, let the images disappear and concentrate on your breathing for a minute or two and then return again to work with visualization for 2 – 3 additional minutes and so on.

Try to work this way for 12 – 15 minutes or stop the exercise when you feel that you cannot concentrate anymore.

It is possible to perform the exercise several times a day.

Remember that you succeed in every action you visualize!

Preparing with such an exercise not only helps you in your mental preparation for the next game, it also improves your ability to transfer from narrow to broad concentration.

Maybe the suggested exercises seem to you in part unrelated. Anyway, I ask you to take my word – the exercise will improve your concentration ability.

Summary

- Concentration is the most important element for your success.
- Every action, even the simplest or the most instinctive, requires concentration.
- Keeping a stable level of concentration during the whole game is a difficult task, but it is your goal.
- Lack of concentration, even for a short interval; is your enemy.
- Concentration is defined as the ability to pay attention for a long time to information important for the game, while disregarding any other information.
- There are two types of concentration: narrow concentration and broad concentration.
- The ability to transfer quickly and efficiently between the two of them is essential for your success.
- Concentration is influenced by lack of confidence and from lack of emotional control.
- When concentration wanders in the direction of the past or when a thought about the past arises (everything that happened before the game or any action that was already performed in the game), your concentration in the present is hurt. In other words, what you are trying to perform in this moment.
- When concentration wanders in the future or a thought about the future occupies you (everything that will happen after the game), your concentration in the present is damaged.
- Too broad concentration makes you process irrelevant information and disturbs your concentration.

- Concentrating on your body and pain hurts your concentration.

> **Stress is the enemy of concentration.**
> **A player under pressure is always a**
> **player without concentration.**

- Exhaustion and lack of fitness damage concentration. A tired player is less concentrated.
- To improve your concentration, you first need to know what hurts it.
- Control over thoughts, replacing negative thoughts with positive and controlling your emotions will improve your concentration.
- Use keywords and "rituals" to keep and return concentration.

> **Your concentration is situated where your**
> **eyes are looking at. Keep your eyes on the field.**

- In order to be concentrated you should detach from everything that happened before the game or that already happened in the game and from the thoughts and feelings you brought from home.
- To the extent it depends on you, try to practice in the presence of factors that disturb your concentration.
- Your concentration should be only on the present, only on the actions you perform right now.
- Your concentration should be only on the field and on your personal and team duties in the game.
- Mental preparation will help you keep your concentration for a long period of time.

- Concentration ability can be improved with practice.

- Training is the place and time to work and improve concentration.

The Coach Box

If you are concerned with the concentration of the players you should advance this subject in training as well. Actually, it is essential to exploit practice for developing concentration. You can't finish a training session with players lacking concentration. You must require them to concentrate on the present, to keep their eyes on the field, to disengage from previous actions and to concentrate only on performing their duty (you must criticize arguments with the referee in practice games, quarrels between the players etc.).

Concentration during training is an essential condition for improving the players' concentration ability throughout the game. If the training conditions are close to the conditions in the coming game and training includes work on concentration as well, the chances are higher that the players will remain concentrated for the whole game. This is especially important if you know from your previous experience that the team has difficulties concentrating in certain conditions like rain, wind, high temperatures, a night game, a huge crowd, etc.

It is true that you cannot train in the exact conditions that will exist in the game. However, when this is technically possible it is advisable to train in these conditions.

One of the factors that hurts the players' concentration is the absorption of too much information. When the ball reaches a player, there are immediately at least eight advisors who tell him what to do with it (the crowd is yelling, the bench is giving instructions and of course the players next to him).

It is true that you do not have control over the crowd, but you can control the "advisors" from the bench and the other players. You should insist from your players to play silently and from the bench to shout as little as possible. Anyway, only one person is allowed to give instructions and that is you. **You must require from the players that except in cases where they have to warn a player who does not see an opposing player (like when he is coming from behind), they should not give instructions to the player with the ball.**

On the one hand, this sounds absurd, because when you ask the players they will tell you that the shouting of the other players bothers them. On the other hand it does not prevent them from yelling when somebody else has the ball.

Like the players you are also only human and concentration is an important factor for your success and decision making. All the factors that disturb the concentration ability of the players hurt your concentration as well and especially stress.

When you are under pressure (and when are you not?) your concentration ability is hurt and as a result your ability to understand and analyze what is happening on the field and to make the best judgment is weakened as well. That's why it is important that you learn to cope with this kind of stress. This will not only turn you into a healthier man, but will also allow you to be a better coach.

The last subject I want to speak about is injury. As we said, a player concentrated on his body, pain or fear of being hit again is a player lacking concentration who will make mistakes.

I don't know why, but coaches and the media praise injured players who continue to play or players who start the game with an injury and play with pain and refuse to be replaced.

In most cases the best for the injured player and the team is for him to sit, even if he does not like it. There are enough games that are decided because of mistakes of injured players. This is not to say that you can't ask a player to overcome his pain and to show his full capability, but only on one condition, that he does not endanger his health and you are sure he can ignore the pain.

Just one more thought: if your injured player in his condition is better than his substitute, you have a problem!!!

Think before you decide not to replace an injured player.

Chapter 20 – Injuries are Part of the Game

Step 16 : Use Your mental power to cope with Injuries

What is common between injuries and the mental aspects of the game?

If you are wondering why I dedicate a whole chapter to write about injuries in a book dealing with the psychology of soccer, then we have a problem. In this chapter I will try to teach you to see injuries in a different way and to treat them.

These are the goals of the chapter:
- **To understand that there is a relation between our mental state and the chances to get injured.**
- **To understand that injury always harms our mind (even when your leg is injured).**

Every Injury Is Also A "Head" Injury

- **To understand that in the process of recovering from an injury it is important to treat the injury to your mind as well.**
- **To understand that mental work can expedite physical and mental recovery.**
- **To understand that pain too is part of the game.**

Every one of us knows enough cases of players who ended their career because of a single injury. This is not to say they did-n't recover from the injury. On the contrary, their body recovery was perfect, however when they returned to play they did not succeed in recapturing the ability they had before the injury. This fact exemplifies the degree to which injury is always more than only a body injury.

One more example describing this fact exists in players who tend to get injured. Almost in every team there is at least one player who gets injured more frequently than the other players playing in his part in the team or in other teams. Usually, he is not a very aggressive player and from the first sight there is no explanation, for why he gets injured more than the others. Sometimes we explain this with a lack of fortune, bad luck or certain superstition. However, if we check the mental state of these players in many cases we will find that the injury is based on mental factors.

An additional example is the difference in the recovery time of players with the same kind of injury. We expect that a fracture in the leg is the same fracture in different players and from a physical point of view there should not be a significant difference in the recovery time of athletes with similar fractures. In reality, there are athletes who amaze the specialists and recover much faster than expected for the type of injury and its severity. Cases like these also demonstrate the fact that the mental work of the athlete is probably the factor that led him to faster recovery.

Mental factors in injury

The injuries in soccer can be divided into two types:

1. Injuries resulting from contact with another player.

2. Self inflicted injuries (springing or tearing of a
   muscle, injuries in the knees because of bad movement,
   injuries resulting from over pressure, over training etc.)

We can see that each of the two types of injury also has specific mental factors. This is easier to understand about self-inflicted injuries, however injuries resulting from contact with another player also are influenced by mental factors. Of course, there always will be injuries we cannot prevent and without any relation to our mind (however we will see later that mental factors influence recovery).

When you try to take a ball from an opposing player or when an opponent tries to steal the ball from you and there is contact between the two of you, somebody might be injured. As we said sometimes this cannot be prevented, but in some of the cases we can point to factors like – **stress, lack of concentration, over motivation, frustration and anger**. They in fact lead to injury. Players who play with exaggerated aggressiveness, because they are trying to prove themselves or a player who has lost the ball and is trying to regain it at any price or a player with over-motivation who is trying to perform a move he cannot. In all these case the result can be a needless injury.

Let's take for example sliding for the ball that is in the legs of an opposing player in an attempt to take it. Sometimes this ends with injury to the foot of the opponent and the result can also be an injury to the player, who is trying to steal the ball. Performing a good slide tackle and taking the ball without a foul requires a high level of concentration and coordination. A player under stress whose concentration is hurt has the least chance of making a clean tackle. Such a player has a higher chance of committing a foul and sometimes of unnecessary injury.

In the same way, a frustrated or angry player (angry at himself, the coach or an opponent player) performs the slide tackle not only with his whole body, but also with his anger. And again the chance to win the ball in such a situation is very slight and it can result in an injury.

Lack of concentration and emotional control are the major mental factors that prevent us from showing our ability and they also lead to injury.

In the second type of injuries (self-injuries) the weight of the mental factors is even higher. The research shows a relationship between the stress level of the player and the chance to get injured.

Stress damages your concentration ability, your coordination, lowers your reaction threshold, hurts your ability to make the right decisions and tightens your muscles. As we saw – all these factors also can lead to injuries and can be the cause of injury.

Over motivation and lack of emotional control are responsible for self-injuries as well. A player with excessive motivation is not always meticulous in getting an efficient warm up and he is trying to perform things that his body can't – actions that lead to self-injury.

A player with excessive motivation tries to prove to the coach that he is capable of being more aggressive and again - too much aggressiveness might end with a wrong move and an injury.

I worked with a player whose coach didn't let him play, because he was not "playing defense". When the player finally had his chance he tried to prove to the coach that he was able to defend. After several minutes in the game he tried to slide for a ball with aggressiveness and determination which resulted in self-injury.

Lack of emotional control is also a factor leading to self-injury. Feelings like anger and frustration that become a part of our actions on the field might lead to injury.

The conclusion – a player under pressure is a player who tends to get injured. Increased pressure also increases the chance for inflicting an injury.

Another case that happens fairly often in soccer is knee self-injury. Such a mishap occurs when a player tries to change the direction of his movement. However, because of lack of concentration he does so with his shoe stuck in the ground. This leads to knee injury.

I hope I succeeded convincing you that mental factors such as lack of concentration, stress, over-motivation etc. might inflict injuries.

In the previous chapters of the book we saw that the same mental factors might prevent you from showing your maximum ability and this was a sufficient reason to work and train on them. Now, you have one more good reason to work on them – preventing needless injury.

What can be done?

If you work meticulously on regulating stress and motivation, emotional control and concentration you will be a better player and a player who does not get unnecessary injuries.

Injury is always injury to the mind as well
When a player gets hurt his injury does not result
only in a physical injury.
Every body injury comes with injury to the mind.
The sudden transition from being an active player to a player
in pain on the bench or at home injures the mind of the
player as well. The intensity and the ability to get over it
changes from player to player,
but it is common to every athlete with injury.
If we manage to understand that every physical injury
is also a mental one we can conclude that together with the
treatment of the body injury we should care for the mental
injury too, if we want to recover and be
the same players as before.

In this chapter I will describe the mental price of injury. Your awareness of mental injuries is the beginning of the solution to the problem. A more complete   solution should be to learn to ask for professional help when needed. Just as you and your teammates have no problem turning to a specialist when you have a body injury, you should decide when necessary to turn to a sport psychologist. It is true that some players succeed in treating the mental element of their injury with their own powers, but they are exceptions. Do not decide immediately that you are one of them.

Although I hope you won't get injured at all, if you are already injured it is worth to have a good check with yourself how you cope with the injury and if it isn't the time to

**integrate in the treatment a consultation
with a sport psychologist.**

The player's reaction to injury

When we check players' reactions to injury we find a lot of things in common:

- The initial reaction right after the injury is **denial**. The player does not believe that this has happened to him. He tends to lessen the meaning of the injury and its severity.
- The second stage is **anger**. Here the player understands the reality of his injury and is angry at himself and at everyone related to him. Sometimes this is reflected in a burst of anger towards his closest family and friends.
- In the next stage the player is busy looking for reasons for the injury. He tries to **explain** why he got hurt, not necessarily reaching the real reasons for the injury. It is much easier to blame the opponent or the quality of the field, than **admit being under pressure, not concentrated and without a proper warm up**.
- The following stage is **depression**. Here the full meaning of the injury is appreciated. The pause in activity for a long period of time and uncertainties about the future create the depression.
- The final stage is a stage of **admitting – accepting**. In this stage the player gets out of depression and is ready to begin concentrating on rehabilitation and returning back to activity.

As I said, most players who get injured go through these stages. The pace and time that it takes a player to pass the stages differs from one player to another and depends on his personality and the support he receives.

Some players will pass the stages in a day or two and then will be able to concentrate on rehabilitation. On the other hand there are those who need weeks or months to go through this process.

Let's hope you won't experience injury, but if you do, it is important to remember that your feelings are normal and what is really important is to accept the injury and to concentrate on rehabilitation.

The problems begin when players remain deep in their depression. Such players will find it extremely difficult to overcome the injury and that is why turning to a psychologist is essential for them.

It is also important to reach the real causes for the injury in the stage of attributing reasons (because this will help you learn from the injury and make it sure that this kind of injury won't happen again in the future), and not to continue blaming everybody except yourself for the injury. **Today we know that taking personal responsibility for the injury** (when this is the real reason)**, will quicken the process of rehabilitation and the return to activity.**

In addition to these stages, physical injuries also bring up some other reactions:
- **A decline in self-confidence**
- **Lower belief in yourself**
- **Fear**
- **Anxiety**

Be aware that these feelings are also normal.

<u>So what do we do when we are injured?</u>
We deny, we are angry, look for reasons, get depressed, however we try as quickly as possible to accept the injury and to understand that injuries are part of sport.

Just as we accept success with love, so should we know to accept the disappointments and to start working on the rehabilitation of our body and mind.

We cannot have only body rehabilitation and hope that the player will return to his ability before the injury. As a player, if you are injured, learn to insist on work on all aspects of the injury – physical and mental. When this work is not done, we see a player who has fully recovered from the physical injury, but does not succeed in recapturing his maximum ability.
If an injury is always an injury in the mind too, its treatment should always include treatment for the mind as well.

Mental work during injury

Combining proper mental work with the treatment of the physical injury shortens the recovery time and rehabilitation. However even more importantly, it allows the player to recover from the injury to return and show his full ability.

The goal of this chapter is to provide you with the mental instruments with which you can cope with physical and mental injury and you will be able to return as fast as possible to full game ability. Knowing this can also assist other players from the team who are injured and haven't read this book. For the best of the team and your personal good, tell them what you have learned.

Mental instruments for dealing with physical and mental injury.

Accepting responsibility

The first stage in dealing with your injury is to accept your responsibility for the treatment of the injury. Your rehabilitation from the physical and mental injury and your return to full play ability is only under **your responsibility**. Even if you are helped by other people like a coach, physical trainer, physician, physiotherapist, psychologist etc – **the responsibility is entirely yours**. Don't transfer the responsibility for the treatment even to a physician, never mind his good intentions.

You are responsible for your injury and you should be a partner to all the decisions about its treatment. Insist on receiving information about your injury!

Usually, as humans, when we seek the assistance of physician we tend to "dwarf" ourselves and to transfer the responsibility for our treatment to the physician. However, for a professional athlete, his body is his career and he can't act this way. The responsibility for treatment is entirely yours. Even when you are injured and on the bench you still must take responsibility for your actions.

Don't hesitate to insist on a second opinion about the process of treatment and rehabilitation, don't hesitate to ask for the best diagnosis equipment (even if you have to pay for it) and don't hesitate to insist on the integration of a sport psychologist into your treatment team. Remember that the responsibility falls only on you!

When you accept the responsibility and after the process of treatment and rehabilitation has been decided with your approval, you are, of course, responsible to follow the treatment. Because of that you should follow and complete the instructions of the treatment team.

Defining goals

Defining goals is important for every athlete, but its importance grows even more especially when you are not playing. In such situations, you define goals for the rehabilitation process and the return to activity.

Defining goals about the rehabilitation process is done together with the treatment team. The goals are yours and you must believe you can achieve them. **Of course you must define realistic goals**.

According to the severity of the injury, you should define short-term goals (for a week, fortnight) and goals for the middle and long term. Remember that there are no sacred goals. The goals exist only to help you with the rehabilitation process. That is why it is necessary always to check how you advance with your goals and to update them accordingly.

The goals are defined based on the professional experience of the treatment team with similar injuries and the average rehabilitation process. **However, your body is not an average body and it is the only one you have**. This is why the average might not fit you. Sometimes your body recovers faster then the average and sometimes slower. That's why it is always important to update the goals throughout the process of rehabilitation.

Remember that only you really know your body and only you feel the pain. Don't try to quicken the process without the agreement or the knowledge of the treatment team. **All your motivation should be directed to fulfilling your goals and not beyond that, even if on a particular day you feel good and you think you are capable of more. You certainly know play-ers who returned to activity too early and the result was a worsening of their injury and lengthening of the rehabilita-tion process**.

Here are some examples of defining goals:

First week – complete rest, taking pills and treatments.

Second week – starting to exercise 10 minutes, and swimming 20 minutes a day.

Third week – continuing with treatment, beginning to run easily 30 minutes.

Fourth week – increasing the intensity and the time of the run without pain.60 minutes including 15 minutes kicking.

Fifth week – gradual return to training with the team.

The goals must be time defined and be clear and specific. There is no sense in general goals where success and completion cannot be evaluated.

After defining goals – it is your responsibility to work for their completion. Don't try to do too much, too fast and too hard. Your main goal now is only to keep your goals.

(as I said it is sometimes possible and necessary to update the goals).

Receiving support

The injured player tends to cut himself from the team. **In cases like that, it is very hard to watch the players playing and practicing while you are unable to do so. However, disengaging from the team only strengthens the tendency to develop depression**.

In fact, the right time to receive support from your team mates is when it is hard for you. Such support is important. It transmits to the injured player that he is not alone and even when he is injured he is still an indispensable part of the team.

> **If you are injured learn to receive the support of others and if a teammate is injured, support him.**

Another important source of support is family and friends. It is true that an injury completely changes the player's family routine and his status in the family changes. From the strong, famous and dominant man in the family the player turns to be the "weak", dependent one. In moments like this he needs the support of his family.

For some of the players this transition is very difficult and strengthens the feelings of anger that come with the injury. A loving and supporting family will help the player recover faster. The family members should know to accept the anger of the player and his low spirit and to understand that his anger is directed towards those closest to him.

An additional important source of support is the work with a sport psychologist when necessary. In addition to his help in the rehabilitation process he can provide you with one more important source of support.

The mental work of the injured player

Some of the things you will read in this chapter may seem to you impossible or illogical. However, I can promise you one thing for sure - if they don't help you they at least won't hurt you.

I believe, and this is based on the experience of many athletes, that mental work is efficient and it quickens the body recovery. It is important that you too believe in that. But even if you don't, try it and give it a chance to prove itself. Don't dismiss it without trying first, because it won't hurt you.

The goal of this chapter is to teach you to exploit your mental powers for quickening your body recovery and simultaneously to work on your mental injury. Such work will lead you to a state in which you will be capable after the recovery to return to the fitness and ability you had before the injury.

The mental work designated for treating the injury is based on the connection existing between the brain and the body and between the thought and imagination and the body. When we dealt with visualization, we deeply emphasized this connection that we will use this time to treat the injury. Even without a full scientific explanation about the way our thought influences our body, what is important for us is that this influence exists and we can use it for good.

The first stage of the mental work is to find your attitude to the injury. The meaning you give the situation will also decide the pace of your recovery. If you treat the injury as a "disaster" or "the end of the world", naturally the results will be developing depression and much slower recovery. That is why it is better to think about injuryin a different way:

It is possible to think about injury as an opportunity to show your courage and determination to recover and return to full ability.

In this way, the recovery becomes a challenge for you.

If you decide that you want to face this challenge with success, the chances will grow that you will meet your goals and that you will return to full activity as early as possible.

Some players take injury as a relief, a solution for lack of success, for bad functioning and frustration. In this way, the injury takes away from them the responsibility and the tension. Such attitude will certainly lead to a longer recovery time.

As an injured player; it is important that after you have calmed down from the initial shock, you check your attitude to your injury.

The second stage of the mental work is more practical. Here you build for yourself a series of short positive sentences that relate to the treatment of your injury. You can use sentences like:

- I succeed in treating the injury.
- I persist with the treatments and keep my goals.
- I become stronger from day to day.
- My body recovers very quickly.
- My injury is disappearing.
- I am positive and believe in fast recovery.

You can fit more specific sentences to your injury ("my fracture is getting better" etc.). Anyway, your goal should be to repeat and memorize these sentences several times a day. You must say them with full intention and belief in their meaning. You can write them on paper and put them in front of you. Even if you have doubts about the efficiency of these sentences, what do you have to lose? **Repeat them several times a day and you will discover how your feelings get better and with it the pace of your recovery.**

Mental training

As I wrote, some injured players detach themselves from their teams. They don't show for training, don't take part in the social activities of the team and don't participate in the team discussions. Some of them even don't come to the game.

I recommend a different attitude. Starting from the first moment the player can drive and walk, it is very important not to be isolated from the team. The player should come to training, should participate in the team activities and discussions. I said earlier that an injured player needs support. **The best source of support for a player – is his team**. It is true that it is not easy to sit on the side and watch your team training and playing. And it is not easy to see the player who got your place in the line-up succeed – because this means that after you recover you will need to compete for your place in the line-up.

Again, you should think positively "My replacement is good for the team. It will be a challenge for me to prove that although I was injured I am a better player than him." This way of thinking will help you achieve the goals you defined and will advance the rehabilitation process, when it is hard for you and it hurts.

Although it is less expected, it will also be hard for you to see your replacement fail, because you might feel guilty and blame yourself about your team's lack of success (even if the thought that it will be easier for you to return to the line-up passes through your mind…).

In cases like these too, you should return to positive thinking and not feel guilty for hurting your team, because you did not get injured intentionally. You can only be blamed if you don't adhere to your treatment and don't recover thoroughly. From this point of view, you should concentrate and transfer the source of guilt into motivation to continue and stand on the goals you have determined.

Beyond receiving support from the team and remaining a part of the team, I recommend you come to training in order to practice.

If you cannot train physically, train with your imagination.

If you come to training or not, you must find time to train using your imagination. Not without a reason, you read and hear interviews with athletes who are seriously injured, but return to compete in the highest levels of sport again, much earlier than expected.

The common thing to all of them was: working with imagination for practice and for treating their injury.

Training with imagination

The goal is to perform with the help of your imagination exactly what the other players perform on the field or in the fitness room.

Close to the weekly training schedule of the team you train with your imagination – **you perform visualization**. Here you use the principles of visualization in order to practice with your imagination. From this point of view, this is the time to go back and read again the chapter dealing with visualization.(chapter 9).

- It does not matter if you are at home or on the field, you choose a place to sit or lie down.
- Concentrate on your breathing for about 2 minutes and start practicing with visualization at the same time your team practices on the field.
- It happens to you right now. You see yourself enter the field. You move freely. You feel your movements. You feel great.
- Now, you begin working with your imagination on the warm up and the stretches. You can see yourself run easily with your teammates. You feel your movements, your muscles. You feel good. You run freely. Nothing obstructs you. Continue this way with your warm up and stretches for a couple of minutes.
- Now, the players begin to play in a circle 5 on 2 (or any other exercise) and you perform exactly the same in your imagination. You concentrate on your feelings and on the movements you perform. Work this way for several minutes.
- The practice continues in different games and exercises and you try to work with your imagination as much as possible. Because it will be difficult for you to continue this way for the whole practice session, take breaks. However, be careful and work on the same exercises as the rest of the players on the field.

You should perform similar work with the game too. Choose a particular time during the week, maybe in the morning before the game and use it for working with imagination for the coming game. Your goal should be to see yourself participate in the coming game. You should feel your movements and body experiences. Because it will be difficult to work with visualization for 90 minutes, you should strive to imagine at least two episodes of 15 minutes.

- Sit or lie comfortably and concentrate for 2 minutes on your breathing.
- It happens to you in this very moment. You feel you are playing. You see yourself enter the field for a warm-up. You see the rest of the players from your team, the grass, the stadium and the crowd.
- You feel it right now. You feel the movements you perform. You feel incredibly good. You have no pain.
- Concentrate on the warm-up for a couple of minutes.
- Now you are playing. It is happening to you. The referee whistles and the game begins.
- Work with visualization on different game conditions and see yourself function properly. Feel the movements of your muscles. You succeed in every action you take. You are good in defense, saving balls with security, aggressiveness and no fear at all. You pass the ball precisely and continue moving all the time. You feel your movements. You feel your body. You join the offense. It happens to you in this single moment. You feel the movement and kick the ball towards the goal. You rise for a header. You feel the movement of your body. You feel the contact between your head and the ball...

In this way you imagine the game. When you feel you are

losing your concentration and different thoughts enter your mind replacing the images of the game, take a break and concentrate on your breathing for about 2 minutes. Afterwards, return and continue working with imagination.

Working with imagination influences:
- **Your body**
- **The connection between your brain and muscles**
- **The muscles themselves**

If you don't train and work with visualization, these connections become weaker. Because working with imagination keeps and strengthens these connections and doesn't let the body "forget" them, you strengthen your ability to transfer from training mentally to the real training and your recovery from the injury will be better and faster. Anyway, **what do you have to lose? You have plenty of free time! Use the time for training and playing in your imagination.**

Treating injury with the help of imagination

Our mind and imagination have capabilities we usually are not aware of. That's why, if we can use these abilities for quickening the recovery process, why not do so? What is there to lose? Why not exploit every resource that can quicken our recovery? Because working with imagination cannot lead to any harm, there is no reason not to combine it in addition to all the other treatments.

Speak with your doctor and physiotherapist and ask them to describe how your injury looks – discover the type of the fracture, how does a stretched or torn muscle look, what happened to your knee, etc. Afterwards, ask them to explain to you what happens in the process of recovery – the fracture is closing, the bone is re-growing etc. and how should the injured place look after full recovery.

- Perform a relaxation exercise of several minutes and afterwards begin treating your injury with the help of imagination – concentrate on the injured place. Look at your wound. Try to see it from all directions, see its form and look deep into it. Feel the injury. Be aware of its existence. The injury is a part of you – part of your body. You have negative feelings about the injury and your body. You are angry about it. You are displeased that your body let you down.

- Let the negative feelings leave you. Concentrate on your breathing. Together with the air leaving you, your anger about the injury and all the negative energy also breaks out. You feel how your anger and negative emotions leave you and make room for posiitive feelings and energies that will help you recover faster.

- Now, concentrate on the injury and bring to your imagination an image of the hurt place, the way it looks after recovery. Look at the image in detail. This is the image you want to transmit to your body.

- Concentrate on the injury and with your imagination release the muscles around the injured place. Let the them remain loose.

- Look in your injury and start treating it with the help of imagination. See how your body generates new cells in place of the damaged ones. See how the blood vessels begin to function again. See in your imagination how the blood flow in the vessels of the injured area becomes steadier. Feel the wound get better. The state of complete and full recovery is getting closer. Remain with this thought for several minutes.

- Now, let the images slowly disappear and concentrate on your breathing. Clear your mind from thoughts and continue concentrating on your breath. Repeat a couple of times with intention the positive sentences you have chosen. You can use sentences like:
    - I succeed in treating my injury.
    - I follow the treatments and stand to my goals.
    - I become stronger from day to day.
    - My body is recovering fast.
    - My injury is disappearing.
    - I am positive and believe in my fast recovery.
- Concentrate now on your breathing and feel how you are filled with positive emotions. You are no longer angry about your injury. You are certain in your complete recovery and in your return to the ability you had before the injury. With all that joy, your belief in your full recovery grows and strengthens. The belief that you fasten the process of recovery becomes stronger too.
- Very slowly open your eyes.

Try to exercise several times a day.
You can help your body expedite the recovery process.
Don't give up the forces you have, learn to exploit them!

Facing the pain

Pain is an inseparable part of dealing with sport. Of course, pain comes with every injury, but not only with injury. During training or a game we also feel pain as a result of a hit, bad movement, muscle spasm, over-activity, etc.

The first and most important stage when dealing with pain is to learn the difference between pains that come from an injury (that if we continue playing we might worsen our state) and pain that comes from body activity, that rest and a break in activity will heal.

Another type of pain is a pain that comes from a chronic body problem. For example, if the cartilage of your knee has eroded and it causes you pain in the knee. This problem cannot always be corrected and you as a player must learn to play with the pain.

The feeling of pain is different for every player. This means that the same injury causes different intensities of pain in different players.

Our ability to function with pain and the type of reaction we have to pain also differs from person to person and depends on many factors. Learn to recognize your pain and know what it tells you "There is an injury" or "It is a result of too much effort".

You are the one who knows your body more than anyone and that's why you should distinguish properly what the pain tells you.
As a player your body is your instrument and you don't have spare parts for it.

You can play with pain when you don't endanger yourself or do not worsen your injury, but only after consulting the medical staff. If you want to show your full ability despite the pain you should learn to cope with it.

Of course the easy and simple solution for dealing with the pain is to use a medicine against it, to use painkillers. Like any other medicine these pills have side effects. Before you begin taking it, try to exploit your mental abilities to lessen the pain. In other words – try to use the natural powers of your mind first.

Pain resulting from an injury

These are cases in which a slight or severe injury causes pain. Together with treating the injury the pain should also be treated and its intensity reduced. Lessening the pain will improve your feelings, will make it easier for you to have a positive attitude about your injury and will give you a chance for a faster recovery.

In this case, the work is not done on the field, but at home or during the physician or physiotherapist's treatment.

- Perform a relaxation exercise for several minutes.
- Concentrate on the place that hurts. Feel the pain. Try to compare the pain to something perceptible. If this is a permanent pain you can compare it to a vise pressing the hurting place. If you suffer from sudden pain you can compare it to a nail and a hammer. The idea is to express the pain with the help of something imaginable that can be changed. I will use the vise as a sample.

- Concentrate on the place that hurts. Use your imagination and start relaxing the muscles in the hurting place. Speak to your muscles and relax them. Feel how the intensity of the pain is diminishing.
- See in your imagination how your body injects more blood into the pain area, how it flows oxygen to the area and weakens the pain. The pain now diminishes.
- The vise pressing the hurting area causes your pain. See the vise in your imagination and feel the pain. Start opening the vise with your imagination. Very slowly you release the pressure, the vise pressure reduces and the pain diminishes.
- Now take several deep breaths and feel the reduction of the pain.
- Continue releasing the vise and feel how it opens more and more and the pain slowly disperses. Feel the pain slowly disappear. The vise is completely open now, your muscles are released and the pain has significantly reduced.
- Concentrate on your breathing and bring to your imagination the injured area, when it will be completely recovered. See yourself move freely without pain.
- Now, let the image disappear, concentrate on your breathing and very slowly open your eyes.

Repeat the exercise several times a day and you will gradually feel how the intensity of the pain reduces, your feelings improve and the recovery process shortens.

Pain before or during a game

A player with pain cannot show his full ability, because naturally when it hurts us our body and mind concentrate on the pain and the result is impaired concentration and poor ability.

In order for a player suffering from pain to show his full ability, he must exploit his mental resources to concentrate in the game and not on the pain.

If you start playing with pain (of course with the permission of the medical staff) try to use the minutes in the changing room before the game to perform relaxation exercises and work on the pain as was described earlier. Tell yourself "I play without pain", "The pain gives me motivation" and similar sentences.

The second important factor is your motivation. It is the key to neutralizing the influence of the pain. When you are ready to play and your motivation is appropriate for your maximum ability (remind yourself from the chapter about motivation) the pain won't bother you.

During the game when you feel pain as a result of a previous injury or because of physical contact during the game the solution is to disconnect from the pain in such a way that you are aware of it and you decide to put it aside.

To achieve this you need to use mainly your breathing. Because during the game you cannot perform relaxation or visualization, it is important to to use your breathing for your benefit. Every time you feel pain or get hit the first thing you have to do is take a deep breath and while blowing it out to tell yourself – "Together with the air the pain also leaves my body".

Returning to play after an injury

Physical injury is always a mental injury too. As a player you certainly know several cases of players who got injured and despite their complete recovery did not succeed to recapture the ability they had before the injury. The reason for this is that treating only the body injury without helping the mental injury does not allow some of the players to really return to their full ability before the injury.

If you behave according to the instructions in the book, it is most probable that your mental recovery will match your body recovery. When you feel that your body fitness and ability to play have reached the levels before the injury and still you do not succeed to recapture your full capabilities, this is the right time to ask yourself why it is happening to you. When you have no physical reason for the decline of your ability, the reason is always in your mind.

The stories of two players

To illustrate to you the importance of the mental side of treating an injury, I will tell you of two players from the premier league. Two real stories! I changed some details to prevent the recognition of the players.

Story one

Let's call him Mike. Mike was a young player, a replacement in a soccer team from the premier league. Mike played as a back midfielder and he began the season on the bench. Mike had motivation and belief in his ability. He invested in training and tried to become a part of the line-up. During the season, because of injuries and other constraints the coach put him in the opening line-up because he had no other options. Mike exploited the chance he had received, showed great ability and won his place in the first eleven.

Mike worked hard in physical and mental training. He showed consistently high ability for half the season. The coaches of the national team noticed him and began talking about him as a future midfielder in the national team.

During a regular training session Mike got injured in his ankle. The injury was serious and grounded him for a month. Of course, he lost his place in the line up.

Mike followed the instructions of the professional staff about everything concerning his recovery and returned to game ability and succeeded in recapturing his full play capabilities.

During training, the coach noticed that Mike had become too "soft". He was trying to avoid body contact and when he was told about it he denied it, insisting that he was playing hard as usual.

Mike did not have any physical problems and because his fitness was great, the coach decided to give him again an opportunity to play. During this game Mike invested great effort, but every time he had to enter a physical confrontation, he didn't go all the way. As a result Mike did not succeed in his duties in defense as a back midfielder despite the fact that he participated successfully in offense. Mike was replaced during the game, because he was a "hole" in the defense.

This continued happening in the training as well. Mike was grounded on the bench and didn't play until the end of the season. Because he was excluded from the team for the following season, he tried to enter a team from the lower league and after several games he got injured again and retired from soccer.

The explanation is clear. Mike treated only his body injury. Mike and the professional staff did not care to treat his mental injury. As a result, despite having no physical problems he was not able to recapture his ability from before the injury. In this way a young player with great potential and future ended his career. The right work for treating the mental injury at the same time with his recovery process would have prevented for sure the final result.

We must note that beyond the personal problem of the player the financial damage to the club as a result of the loss of a young and promising player was certainly considerable.

Story two

Let's call him Jim. Jim was a player, 25 years old, playing in the premier league as a forward. Jim was an excellent player and he was respected as one of the best in the league.

In the course of one of the games Jim got seriously injured in his knee. The injury was at the exact place he was injured the previous season. The injury required complex treatment, surgery etc. and grounded him until the end of the season. The professional staff opinion was that the chances that Jim would return to play were minimal.

Jim took the responsibility for treating the injury on himself.

He demanded consultation with additional doctors, performed precise examinations and with the cooperation of all involved he built a working program for treating the injury and returning to practice and game ability.

Jim insisted on involving a psychologist in the team treating him and his club agreed. Jim defined goals and worked hard to achieve them. The rehabilitation process wasn't easy, neither from the physical nor the mental point of view.

Through the recovery in the difficult moments Jim was on the verge of deciding to retire from soccer, but with the support he received he decided to continue.

Jim appeared in full fitness for the opening training the following season. He immediately distinguished himself with his ability and returned to be the team's best player.

The whole season Jim showed good ability and was invited to join the national team.

Jim treated his injury from all aspects, including the mental aspect. His recovery was complete, from a physical and mental point of view. **As a result he returned to full game ability and continued his career for several more years.**

Summary

- A player under pressure tends to get injured!
- An un-concentrated player tends to get injured!
- Over motivated players tend to get injured!
- A player who does not control his emotions tends to get injured!
- Regulating stress and motivation, keeping concentration and emotional control will not only make you a better player, they will also help you to prevent injury.

- Mental strength is always body strength too!
- **Every body injury comes with a mental injury!**
- Full recovery from injury requires treating both the body and mental injuries.
- An injured player must take full responsibility for his treatment and rehabilitation!
- The player together with the professional team treating him should define goals for complete recovery and recapturing full game ability.
- The injured player must receive support from those around him – family, teammates etc. and not to remain isolated with his injury.
- With the help of mental work it is possible to expedite the body recovery process.
- Work on the mental injury is essential for the full return to game ability.
- When you do not train on the field, practice in your imagination.
- Your thoughts and imagination will help you treat the injury, cope with the pain and return to full ability.

Mental factors might sometimes be a reason for injury. These factors are always part of the injury and might assist you in recovery from an injury.

The Coach Box

As a coach, you should always be aware of the relation between the mental state of the player and his chances to get injured! It is a pity to lose a player because of an injury that could have been avoided. It is better to think twice before putting a player in the line-up when he seems tense or lacking concentration. In this case he is not only incapable of achieving his maximum potential, but also his chances to get injured are high.

Your duty as a coach is to be sure that every injured player receives the best treatment. Even if you personally do not believe in psychology, the mere fact that different players recover from the same injury in a different pace and that there are players who end their career after a single injury, despite their full body recovery, you should ensure that the injured player also treats the mental aspects of his injury. **Today there is no argument in the world of sport and sport-medicine about the importance of mental treatment after injury.**

After the complete body recovery of the player his return to game ability is mainly influenced by mental factors. Only rarely does an injured player return to full ability straight after his body recovery and return to game ability (body fitness, strength, etc.). Naturally, a player after an injury is afraid not to get injured again. His concentration and his decision-making abilities are impaired. As a result the damage to his ability is indispensable.

It is true that some players return from an injury to full game ability without mental work, but they are the exception. It is your duty as a coach to return every injured player as fast as possible to full game ability. You must do so for the player, the team and yourself. You should direct every injured player to a doctor, physiotherapist and sport psychologist. This is not my invention. This is the norm in the world of professional sport.

As a coach it is your duty to make sure that the club doesn't "abandon" an injured player. In the heat of the season, the team and the club tend sometimes to forget the injured players, especially when the injury requires a long rehabilitation process. For the good of the player and the team you must strengthen the connection with the injured player and support him through the whole recovery period.

Constant work on the mental aspects of the game, starting from the training camp and through the whole season, saves injuries. When injuries happen, mental work enables the quickening of the recovery process and the return to full game ability.

Chapter 21 – Fitness, Nutrition and Rest

This book is entirely dedicated to the mental aspects of the game and the more you read it, it seems to you that this is the only important thing. This of course isn't true. In the beginning of the book I wrote and tried to persuade you too, that the mental aspect is not less important than the other elements of the game. This means that the other elements of the game are as important as the mental elements of the game. I mentioned talent, skill and physical ability.

About talent, things are clear and we won't speak about it in the confines of this book. At this time, I will warn again the players who think that their talent is the most important thing. Such thinking might end their career earlier than expected and without fulfilling their entire potential.

Talent is a very important and essential factor for success, but talent without physical or mental ability and without developing skills won't lead these players much success.

Skill is entirely the result of training and game experience. In different parts of this book I emphasized the importance of training on all aspects of the game.

The most distant area from mental ability, at first sight, is physical ability. I include in body ability the following factors:
- Body size (height, etc.)
- Strength
- Speed
- Quickness
- Fitness

What is common between them and mental ability?

It is true that if you are an adult player you can't change your body structure. However, the other elements of body strength are directly related to mental strength.

The starting point lies in:

> **It is not important how mentally strong you are or the level of your talent and skills, if you don't have the necessary body fitness to demonstrate them from the first minute to the final whistle of the game.**

I am not a fitness trainer and I do not have a method to work on fitness with visualization, in place of sweating in training. The goal of this chapter is only to bring to your awareness the importance of body fitness, nutrition and rest.

Step 17 : Fitness is only your responsibly!

Body fitness

Body fitness is not only the ability to invest effort for a long time. It is also the basis that allows you to demonstrate your potential throughout the whole game and every game.

The relationship between body fitness and mental ability is very close:

- An exhausted player makes mistakes.
- An exhausted player cannot keep maximum concentration.
- An exhausted player commits unnecessary fouls and tends to get injured.

- An exhausted player cannot follow the instructions of the coach.
- An exhausted player cannot express his motivation.
- An exhausted player cannot benefit from his mental strength.
- An exhausted player is not only unable to give his full ability to the team – he might even harm it.

We all know that in the last minutes of the half and of the game a lot of goals are scored relative to the rest of the game. The reasons for this are written in front of you.

Exhausted players > are not concentrated > mistakes – goals are scored

As I mentioned earlier, I don't have, unfortunately, a mental method to work on body fitness. **My goal is only to persuade you that body fitness is your problem! This is not the responsibility of the coach or the team's fitness trainer.**

Body fitness is your problem only!
You are responsible for your body fitness!

It should be clear for a professional player that his body is his instrument and it must be working 100%.

Many players do not love the physical training and this makes it even more important to deal with the subject.

Everyone who visits team training always sees the players who try to take the short path when the coach does not see them. They try not to perform the exercise until the end, do not execute it with maximum speed or for no particular reason "forget" to count and shorten the exercise a bit.

Another problem in some of the teams is that fitness training is done only during the team training and the players do not have personal training schedule.

No doubt the team training is important, but its disadvantage is that it suggests that all the players have the same level of body fitness and that players at the age of 17 train exactly as the 35 year old players of the team.

The result might be that the 17-year-old has the same body fitness as the 35-year-old (if it can be the opposite it would be much better).

When I say that body fitness is your problem and you are responsible for your body fitness, this means that you must insist from your coaching staff a personal fitness-training program beyond the team training.

Because you best know your weaknesses, you must be responsible to work and overcome them. **Of course it is not enough to determine a training program. You should also follow it and here again it is entirely under your responsibility.**

The personal-training program in most cases will be done while the coach or the fitness trainer do not see you (personal work in the fitness room, long runs, working on the field after the end of training, etc.

**The decision is only yours and the
responsibility falls only on you!**

Persistence in the work to improve your body fitness is the key to your success. It is true that it is hard to persevere. You will always have good reasons to prefer to sit on the sofa before the TV and not go out for a run or to the fitness room.

The work on body fitness should be an inseparable part of your soccer life. This is the only way to persist.

It would be best, if you enjoyed working on your body fitness, but that is not what is expected from you. You owe yourself the body fitness training, even if you do not enjoy the practice. And I have no doubt that you will enjoy the results for the long run.

Build a training program together with the coaching staff and define for yourself goals for the short term (several weeks), middle term (several months) and the long term.

The satisfaction of achieving your goals will push you to continue and train more. Anyway, you do not have to work alone. On the contrary, it is desirable to work with another player from the team who has a similar training program.

Try also to diversify your training (do not always run at the same course, change the exercises, etc.). You can listen to music while training (you can also sing) and do anything that will help you persist in performing your training program.

**The work on your body fitness never ends.
As long as you are an active player you must
continue training your fitness.**

Your goal is to be in the maximal body fitness according to your training schedule, according to the part of the season, to your age and more.

**Fitness is a profession! Don't make decisions
on your own, seek professional assistance.
The wrong practice might harm you!**

The work on your body fitness does not end with the end of your fitness session. It has two not less important additional aspects – rest and nutrition, as will be described next.

Rest

At first sight, rest is the opposite of working on body fitness, but it is not true.

Rest is an indispensable part of developing body fitness.

Just as your muscles need effort in order to develop, they need rest too. I am not a fitness trainer and not a sport physiologist. **My goal is only to convince you that exactly as body fitness is under your responsibility, so is rest.**

Step 18: Rest is a part of fitness training. Only you can be responsible for your rest.

It may sound strange that I have to convince you to rest, but experience teaches that some players who work hard on their body fitness don't treat their need to rest with the same importance.

Rest is essential for the revival of your body and muscles and without sufficient rest you won't be able to express your maximum body fitness.

In sports in which effort is invested for the whole game like soccer, the importance of rest is even greater. You practice with effort almost every day, often you play twice a week and if you are in the national team the vacation between the seasons is usually shorter.

Your body needs rest exactly like it needs effort.

When you began your way as a young player your coach probably tried to check when you went to sleep and if you went out late the night before a game. He tried then to teach you the right habits, but in many cases this turns out to be a game of detectives and thieves (when you try to cheat your coach).

The responsibility for your REST is entirely yours!

The coaching staff cannot be responsible for your rest. The coaching staff can control the amount of effort you invest in training (according to the amount of work needed in training). The coaching staff takes for granted that you take the rest you need.

The responsibility to rest is completely yours. Only you can decide if you rest enough to allow your body to revive from the effort. Consult with the professional staff and decide on a personal program not only about body fitness training but also about personal rest.

Just as the work on your body fitness must become an integral part of your sport life so should rest too. Rest is part of your athletic life style.

Just as some players find it difficult to work on their body fitness, there are those who have difficulties resting. The problem is that you must rest even if you do not feel tired. **As we will see in the following chapter, rest is essential for your muscles and it has no relation to being tired.**

Sometimes, and especially after victory, you feel full of energy and you feel like going out to dance the whole night. This is a result of substances that are secreted in our body and influence our brain causing a good feeling.

However, if you "ask" your muscles what they want they will beg you for some rest. Of course, you are not a monk and you do not live in a monastery. You should know how to celebrate, but you have to do so with moderation and receiving sufficient rest after the celebration.

As I wrote rest must be a part of your soccer lifestyle and that's why it does not concern only you, but influences your whole family. It does not matter if you are young and live with your parents or you have your own family.

If you are married or have a girlfriend, rest should be part of your lifestyle. To prevent fights and quarrels it is important to speak with your loved ones – parents, wife, girlfriend, friends – about the way of life the sport requires from you.

Everyone should understand that every professional must care for his instruments, you must guard your body.

Nutrition

The third element of your body ability is nutrition. Your body resembles a very advanced vehicle. If you would like to achieve the best results from it you will have to give it the best treatment and of course the highest quality fuel.

If you want your body to function at its maximum level it needs the treatment of:

- **Body fitness**
- **Rest**
- **Fuel – Right Nutrition**

If you do not give your body the fuel – the most suitable nutrition, maybe you won't have problems in your regular activities, but when you need to invest maximum effort, your body might not function on the expected level (the engine fails and might even stop).

As an athlete you require great efforts from your body at almost every training session and certainly every game. That's why proper nutrition is essential to prevent your body from "failing". **Bad nutrition, beyond the fact that it will not allow you to achieve your maximum ability, also increases the chances for injury and lengthens the recovery period after an injury.**

Step 19 : You kick, head,jump and run for the ball with what you eat.

Every one of us has eating habits and beliefs about the food we eat and we all believe we eat right. Actually, it is not true. When we check thoroughly the players' eating habits we find that most of them (not only soccer players) do not eat right and this hinders them from expressing their full potential.

The food you consume can be the difference between a win and a loss. At the end of the game with your body entirely exhausted it needs energy.
In the last attack of the game, when you are running with the ball towards the goal, you depend on your balanced eating – if your body does not betray you and is capable of performing the commands of the brain even in the 90th minute – this is the real test!

Food is more than a substance that satisfies our hunger. Food is fuel that is composed of different nutritional elements that are essential for our body and allow it to function maximally.

Athlete's nutrition is an independent science today and I have no pretension to teach you correct nutrition.
I write about it for two reasons:

- There is a relationship between mental and physical ability. When your body is physiologically ready for the effort and you have trust and belief in your body, you will be a better player. The right physiological preparation is the basis for good mental preparation. **You can take the most correct decisions and be in the best possible mental state, but if your body is not capable of executing what you command it in a specific moment, the result will be failure.**

- Exactly like body fitness and rest – **the correct nutrition is your problem! You are the only one responsible for it!**

Sport nutrition is a science and every self-respecting club must consult with a certified nutritionist for building a nutrition plan for its players on a general basis and specifically for every player, according to his needs.

If the club does not employ a nutritionist I recommend you to talk with one even on private terms. The price you will pay for his advice will be insignificant to the benefits you will achieve from correct nutrition. This advice is true for every age, for the young and for the experienced player.

The responsibility for having the right nutrition is entirely yours!

Nobody can be responsible for you. The club should help you, but the responsibility is yours (when you sleep in a hotel before a guest game, the club will arrange to order food suitable for you. It is nice and good, but what does it help if you also have to eat the food your mother has prepared for you?).

Correct nutrition is exactly like working on body fitness and rest – it should become an integral part of your life-style, if you want to prolong your career, to show maximum ability and to remain healthy while you are playing and after you retire from professional sport.

Correct nutrition is not only your life-style, it also influences your entire family. **Somebody has to prepare your food, hasn't he?** It is important to explain to your family the requirements from your food and especially to those who are responsible for preparing the food. I am sure that all of them have good intentions and for sure your mom and granny, but it is still possible, without hurting anyone, to direct them to help you eat right. For example, if *pasta* (or any other food)is the secret element, you can certainly ask, that instead of having it every Saturday at 3 PM a couple of hours before the game to eat it Friday night.

What is the difference?

Saturday it will make you heavy. However, on Friday evening the carbohydrates will be absorbed by your body and will help you in the game. I am not a nutritionist and you won't receive from me a recommended diet. However, it is important to remind some of the accepted principles in sport nutrition:

- **The first principle is the most important of all. It is necessary to work with a professional nutritionist!**
- A player must keep stable the optimal body fat percentage and body weight according to the instructions of a professional.
- **A rise in weight, even the smallest one, hurts your fitness**. If you weight 70 kg. a rise of 3 kg. (a mere 4%) does

not sound so bad and I am also sure you will still look good at this weight. **But for your fitness and ability, this is absolutely terrible.**

Imagine yourself running for 90 minutes while you are carrying a 3 kg pumpkin on your back...

This is the effect of gaining weight.
The responsibility for your weight is entirely yours!

- Building the correct nutrition requires deciding on a diet for every day, for the day before a game, for the day of the game and after it.
- When we talk about nutrition it includes drinks as well. Your body requires liquids to function. When exerting physical effort (intensive training or a game) a player weighing 70 kg might lose over 4 liters of liquids (about 6% of body weight). It is your responsibility to return these liquids to the body. If you ask how much you have to drink, the simplest answer is to check the color of your urine. If your urine is not clear and transparent this is a sign that you are still lacking liquids, even if you do not feel thirsty.
- **Warning!** The demands from the players' diet leads sometimes to the development of **eating disorders** (problems like compulsory exaggerated eating followed by self-induced vomiting or using laxatives to prevent adding weight or a drastic fall in weight). **Without treatment,**

eating disorders may lead to unexpectedly severe results. Be attentive to yourselves and to your friends from the team. If you have the suspicion that you or any one from the team has eating problems, report this as early as possible.

**Players diet is not a punishment.
You can definitely develop a menu that is tasty and answers the needs of your nutrition.
Bon appetite!**

Summary

- Your body is your instrument and you have no spare parts for it. You must keep your body so you can always express your full potential.
- **Working on your body fitness is your own problem and only you are responsible for the condition of your body**. Insist on developing a personal body-training program and follow its execution.
- Rest is essential for your body, just like body fitness. **Finding the rest you deserve is your own problem and only you are responsible for getting it!**
- **The right nutrition is an essential condition for the professional player**. Insist on working with profession als in the field and decide on a menu that will fit your needs. **Correct nutrition is your own problem and you are the only one responsible for your diet!**
- Working on body fitness, rest and correct nutrition is an indispensable part of your athletic life-style **and only you are responsible for them! If you persist with them they will help you to be an active player for a**

long time and will guarantee that you will be healthy after you retire as well.

- Eating disorders are a very serious matter. Report them as early as possible!

Body strength is also mental strength –
A healthy mind in a healthy body!

The Coach Box

The subjects related to body fitness, rest and nutrition should be advanced in every team without any doubt. Unfortunately, this is far from reality in soccer around the world. There are no shortcuts in professional sport and there are fundamental elements that cannot be denied. **Body fitness, mental strength, rest and nutrition are fundamental for building a player. The power of these elements will decide the stability of the whole structure.** As a coach you certainly want to give your team the best of everything, but you also have your constraints. It is your duty to try to convince the team owners of the importance of working with professionals and of their financial worthiness. The benefit of their services will always be greater than the price they are paid.

Even when you do not have professionals at your service, you are still responsible to bring to the awareness of the players the importance of working on body fitness, rest, balanced diet and mental strength and you have to help them with all the means you have.

Chapter 22 – Special Game Conditions

In this chapter I will try to bring to your awareness the importance of mental work in special game conditions, like the first minutes of the game, the end of the half, the halftime, the opening of the second half, the final minutes of the game, static situations, scoring a goal, allowing a goal, a mistake by a player, sending off of a player, an injury to a player or yourself. The goal is to exploit the special game conditions for your and the team's benefit, to make less mistakes and to take advantage of your opponent's mistakes. In principle, the team coach should work with his team and prepare it for special conditions, but every single player can prepare and help his team as well.

Step 20 : Exploit special game conditions

The Opening of the Game

As we saw in the chapter dealing with stress, contrary to the belief of many coaches and players stress does not disappear when you enter the field. Only its symptoms change. The clearest indication of stress is lack or impairment of concentration and the result – **a higher number of mistakes in the first minutes of the game and allowing goals, due to defensive mistakes or failing to score because of mistakes by the forwards.**

> **A goal you give up or a goal you don't score in the first minutes of the game because of lack of concentration often changes the whole game.**

To prevent this you must take the field with your level of stress suited to your maximum ability. The right practice and mental preparation are the only solution for this. There is no magic potion! With the importance of the game rising it is your duty to guarantee that you are entering the field with the suitable level of stress.

Even if you do not succeed in regulating the pressure and your stress level is too high when the referee opens the game, you must be aware of it and act accordingly – you should perform simple and not complex actions (make sure passes, dribble less and do not take chances). You should invest great physical effort and at the same time take several deep breaths, tell yourself a couple of encouraging words and only gradually with the decrease in tension return to your usual play.

When you are aware of the influence of stress at the start of the game it is your obligation to try and help the other players as well. Try to calm them down and ask them to play simply and confidently.

The End of the Half

Lack of concentration is caused not only by stress, but also by exhaustion and nagging thoughts. Close to the end of the half you are tired and thoughts like – "When will the referee whistle?", "The next attack is the last one", "When will this half end?", rise in your mind. **These thoughts and the fatigue will impair your concentration ability. As a result the number of mistakes will rise close to the end of the half.**

You should be conscious about this and you should keep your concentration and continue playing all the time at the same level of intensity. Whenever possible take several deep breaths, turn every thought that enters your mind to a motivating idea that helps you continue and invest and disregard everything happening around you.

Halftime

The half time is meant not only for physical rest, but for mental rest as well. You should prepare for the second half exactly like you prepared for the game:

- Take a couple of minutes of mental and physical rest.
- Close your eyes and breathe deeply.
- Concentrate on your breathing and clear your mind from all thoughts for several minutes.

The coach usually will point out your mistakes and will give instructions for the second half of the game. Try to recapture the half for yourself as well. Check what worked for you and what didn't. Think how you can perform your role better in the second half.

Two minutes before leaving the changing room:

- Close your eyes again.
- Take several deep breaths.
- Visualize possible game conditions in the second half.

This mental preparation will raise your self-confidence and the belief in your ability and will regulate your stress level.

The opening of the second half

The opening of the second half is similar to the opening of the game, and you should act in the same way until you match your stress level and fit in the game.

The final minutes of the game

The final minutes of the game are similar to the last minutes of the half, but the intensity is much higher, the exhaustion is greater and your thoughts bother you more (you think about the result "What if we lose?" or "What if we win?", "What will happen if they score right now?" etc.). At this moment an impairment in your concentration might cost you much more and it is not a surprise that relatively more goals are scored in the last minutes of the game.

It is important to be aware of what is happening to your body, about the thoughts passing through your mind and about the way your concentration is influenced. Take a deep breath whenever you can, tell yourself you are playing to the final whistle, give yourself a burst of motivation with every breath you take and try to raise the intensity of your play, especially in the final minutes.

You believe in victory with no dependence on the score. While the game is still on you invest maximum effort and keep the level of your concentration and motivation.

Static conditions

In one of the World Cup Championships research was done about how most of the goals were scored. The results showed that more than 60% of them were scored out of static situations (a penalty kick, a free kick, etc.) or the goal opportunity appeared after a static situation (a heading after a corner, a pass from a free kick etc.).

Even though this is a fact, **the effort coaches invest in practicing static conditions is mostly insignificant**. The team must practice not only **how to score from such situations** (and this is practiced more if still not enough), but also **how not to allow**

a goal from either your own set play or that of your opponent.

Not without intention I emphasized the need to practice how not to allow a goal especially in your own team is static situation. In many cases the result of such situations is a goal for the opponent.

In most teams it is accepted that the stopper (usually a tall player) move forward on a corner kick. Often, immediately after the corner the opponent starts a fast break which leads to a goal due to the depleted defense.

As a player you should prepare yourself for any of these situations, according to your role on the field. Your goal must be to take advantage of the static situations and to prevent the other team from exploiting them for its good.

Free kicks

As I mentioned too many goals are scored from free kicks. A good free kicker is priceless for his team. It is not necessary that the player scores directly. It is enough to pass a precise ball to another player (like on a corner).

The free kick is a skill and it is necessary to practice it as much as possible. In the chapter dealing with visualization I tried to convince you that visualization might help in improving the precision and the strength of a kick and in the accurate execution of set plays.

If you are a free kicker, you have enough time before performing the kick to:

- Close your eyes for a second.
- Decide where to kick the ball.
- Visualize the kick exactly as you would like it to be.
- Feel your movement and see the ball go in the

desired direction.

- Open your eyes and kick the ball with full belief
in your success.

The whole preparation for the kick will take you less then half a minute. Try to use this technique and see your ability improve. If your team uses exercises with free kicks (and I certainly advise this) perform the exercise as planned (visualize before the kick). The exercise is important also for the team consolidation. Often you can see that the whole team prepares for the free kick (players advance to the penalty area etc.) and then the kicker aims directly at the goal, without any chance for success.

Such behavior, when happening several times in a game doesn't only miss the opportunity, but might also damage the team. It is fine if the kicker decides to surprise everyone from time to time. However, in principle a set play should be executed as planned in most of the opportunities.

Preparing for a free kick should be done by all the players and not only by the kicker. Before the ball is in the air visualize the action you want to perform (jumping for a header, a movement, capturing a loose ball etc.). If there is a team exercise visualize your role in it. The players remaining in defense should also prepare for the free kick and the actions that might follow it (sudden attack, etc.).

The players must prepare for a free kick when the ball is in the possession of the other team as well. In this case visualize your defensive role and be prepared to act after the kick too (starting an attack or rearranging the defense).

The right actions of the whole team in a free kick will help to achieve the best from the situation and will lessen the number of goals the team allows from free kicks.

Penalties

At first sight, a penalty kick should be an easy task for a skilled player. The distance is short, there are no defenders, the goal is big, etc. A person who is not acquainted with the mental aspects of the game will predict that at least 90% of all penalties lead to a goal. In fact, this is not true and even in the European Championship we saw missed penalties that decided the champion. In one season of the Premium Israeli League 40% of the penalties were missed.

The problem arises because a penalty isn't performed only with the foot. A penalty is kicked with the "head" too. Without exception, all the missed penalties result from the kicker's head.

Every one has heard the saying – "There is no good penalty goalkeeper, there is only a bad penalty kicker!" and this is the truth. Of course, we all know goalies with relatively high penalty save rates, however these goalies also succeed in saving the penalties, because of the poor performance of the kicker. We will speak about the goalkeeper in the following chapter. Now, let's deal with the player behind the ball.

It is a scientific fact that a powerful kick to the upper corner of the goal from 11-meters cannot be stopped! The velocity of the ball compared to the quickness of the goalkeeper and his reactions do not allow him to stop the ball, even if he "cheats" a bit with a leap.

<u>Basically there are two types of penalty kicks</u>:

1. A strong kick to a corner the kicker had decided (he does not look at all at the movement of the goalkeeper).

2. A kick after diversion or after the goalkeeper has moved.

Of course, both methods are effective, but I think the first type is preferable, because it is less influenced by mental factors.

<u>Why do we miss penalties?</u>

In fact, you already read the answer in the previous chapters. All the mental aspects of the game find expression in a penalty kick. The more significant reasons for the miss are:

stress and lack of concentration.

Stress impairs concentration, but because of its body expression it will also hurt the technical execution of the penalty (muscle spasm, bad coordination etc.).

Concentration is also impaired because of any of the following reasons:

- A tense player is not concentrated on the game.
- A player without belief in success is not attentive.
- A player whose mind is wandering away from the penalty is not concentrated.
- A player indulging in the past ("This goalkeeper already stopped my ball once" etc.) is not concentrated.
- A player dreaming about the future ("We won the game", "I will hold the cup" etc.) is not concentrated

- A player whose concentration is too broad (when kicking a penalty concentration must be centered only on the ball, the goalkeeper and the goal. A player listening to the crowd, sees as well the cameras, the journalists, the audience, etc.) is not concentrated.

How to prevent this?

A player who wants to score from a penalty must develop his mental ability so when he is standing behind the ball his concentration, self-confidence and belief in success will be at their maximum!

Be aware of the following factors:

- **Choose the way you prefer to kick the ball** – a strong kick in one of the corners, preferably a high one, or a kick after diversion and the goalkeeper has moved. As I said I recommend the kick in the corner.

- **Invest in training**. You must reach technical excellence for performing penalties. With your kick becoming perfect your self-confidence will grow and the chances to miss will drop. You must practice kicks to both corners and different heights.

- **Try to put some pressure to the training**. Bet with the **goalkeeper**, place both goalkeepers in the goal and have a competition with them, etc.

- **Practice penalties the whole season**, not only before a National Cup Game.

- **In a game before a penalty (you have enough time) perform a short "ritual" (a series of**

actions) that will include sentences you tell yourself. The ritual can be absolutely private and no one from the other team should see or hear it. Then take several deep breaths, decide where to kick the ball, visualize it exactly as you would like it to happen and send the ball into the net. You perform the penalty with com plete belief in your success!

- **You should train in exactly the same manner.**

- In case you are flooded by thoughts about the past or the future, or you feel you won't succeed in keeping your concentration, take some more time. Breathe deeply, talk to yourself, stop any thought not connected to the present, take several more deep breaths and repeat your ritual before you kick the ball.

- If you decide to kick the ball with diversion or after the goalkeeper has moved, you should work in a similar way.

- In any type of kick you should remember that goal-keepers try to learn how you kick the ball. You must diversify and not kick to one corner only etc.

Scoring a goal

Whenever your team scores a goal this is a happy moment, However, after the deserved joy the goal of every player right after scoring the goal and several seconds of happiness must be **immediately to return to full concentration.**

When a player is overcome by joy and is not in control of his emotions, the result is a loss of concentration. **Everyone**

dealing with soccer knows that too many goals are scored in the 5 minutes after scoring or allowing a goal.

A team that rejoiced for too long does not return to the game fully concentrated, makes mistakes and as a result gives up a goal. This happens to the best of teams and players. **Your goal as a player is to return immediately to full concentration and help the rest of the players do so as well.** After scoring a goal – express your positive feelings, take several deep breaths, talk to yourself and recapture the control over your emotions and concentration.

> **When the game starts again you must be completely concentrated in it.**

If you see that the rest of the players have not yet returned to full concentration try to stop the game. Kick the ball out, commit a foul far from the goal in order to stop the game. All this to allow a few more seconds for your teammates to calm down.

You should practice this situation and the rapid return to emotional control and concentration. Use every situation in practice or friendly games and in training to exercise the return to concentration after scoring a goal. It is also important that the coach as well exercises this subject with the whole team.

You can take advantage of the situation after the opposing team has allowed a goal to try to immediately score one more, but this requires teamwork and the coach's decision.

> **The real joy can be only after the final whistle. Exaggerated joy easily turns into sorrow!**

Allowing a goal

Actually the situation after allowing a goal is similar to the state after scoring a goal. Of course, now we speak about sorrow, anger, frustration etc. contrary to the joy we feel after scoring. However, the problem remains the same – **emotional control and rapid return to full concentration.**

When this does not happen, we can see a team that immediately after allowing a goal in less than 5 minutes gets one more. **Players who bury themselves in sadness are not completely concentrated on the game and the result is – mistakes that might lead to another goal.**

It is necessary to practice this situation as well and to know what to do after allowing a goal (as we saw earlier, it is possible to exploit the lack of concentration of the opponent to try and score a fast goal in return. It is necessary to train even if the coach does not like to talk about what you do after giving up a goal). **On the personal level of every player, the goal should be to achieve immediately complete concentration It is important to preserve self-confidence, belief in personal and team ability, to climb back from lagging behind and win the game.**

Right after allowing a goal, take several deep breaths, recognize your feelings, but with the help of your deep breathing and self-talk, recapture your emotional control. Return to full concentration and strengthen your motivation in order to help your team. Try to cheer up and calm the players around you with the goal – "We will work harder and will return from falling behind".

In case you recognize a lack of concentration in you or the other players, try to postpone the game as much as possible (kick the ball out, commit a foul far from the goalkeeper, etc.) in order to win some more precious seconds.

A mistake made by you or another player

Mistakes are part of the game – every player makes them during the game. The goal is, of course, to lower their number to a minimum. Some mistakes lead to immediate damage, like a mistake of a stopper, goalkeeper, etc. and there are other mistakes that are easily forgiven, like the mistakes of a forward.

The most important goal after making a mistake is to forget about it as fast as possible, without losing concentration, self-confidence and belief in ability.

When you commit a mistake, recognize it immediately and sign with your hand – "My mistake", take a deep breath, tell yourself "Get out of it, come on you can do it..." etc.

Your goal – to disconnect from the mistake and concentrate on what is happening right now in the game. The mistake, regardless of how painful it was, belongs to the past – it is already done!
If you do not forget the mistake it will influence you the rest of the game and will cause you to lose concentration and make additional mistakes.

When your teammate makes a mistake (and it is not important how serious the mistake is and its result), you should try to forget about it and return to the game with full ability.

The entire team yelling at the **goalkeeper** for making a mistake and allowing a goal doesn't serve any purpose. It merely shakes his concentration, self-confidence and the belief in his personal ability not to make anymore mistakes.

This of course is not what you want. The players are angry and frustrated, but they must react completely differently. They should approach the **goalkeeper** at the first opportunity (some players tend to go away from a player who has committed a mistake and to leave him alone – one more reaction without any use for the team). They must encourage him with a word, make him feel they are with him even when he makes mistakes and tell him "Come on! Concentrate! We will win this game!" etc.

As a player, when somebody from your team makes a mistake, take a deep breath, control your feelings (stop yourself from yelling at him) and try to remain positive. Do not make a scene for the crowd or the bench. Give a sign to the player if he is far away and if he is next to you encourage him and forget together that the mistake ever happened and continue forward.

Of course, a player who made a mistake must be held responsible for it and most certainly must learn from it, but this should be done during halftime or after the game. It is the coach's right to replace a player who made a mistake. However, here as well the substitution must be done thoughtfully and not as a result of a burst of emotions (anger, etc.).

A good team is a team whose players know that they can make mistakes. It is possible to try to pass the ball between 8 players and not succeed. It is forbidden to do the same pass in your penalty area. A defender must help in offense, however he must be sure that someone backs him up when he is in attack and not to do this in a situation when all the midfielders and the defense are offense as well.

In a good team players know to recognize their own mistakes and those of the other players and continue without

hurting their team play, concentration, self-confidence and the belief in personal and team ability.

An injury

Injuries are part of the game, but they should not influence you. When a player is injured if you cannot help him stay away and let the medical team treat him. Take advantage of the pause in the game, take several deep breaths, try to balance your emotions (you are worried about the injury, about your friend, however this does neither help him nor your concentration), keep your self-confidence, etc. Exploit the short break for a mental "shot of courage". If there are a couple of team players next to you, you can gather for a few seconds and cheer up each other strengthening your team consolidation.

Sending off a player

When a player from your team is sent off, the natural reaction is anger (usually about the referee, but sometimes about the player who had left the game or the players from the opposing team). **The anger and the emotions that occupy you after the player has been expelled take the team out of concentration and might lead to a much greater damage than the expulsion itself.**

Your reaction as a player should be control over your emotions and converting the anger into positive motivation for investing greater effort. Take a couple of deep breaths, control your emotions and thoughts and push forward. If there are other players around you, calm them down, encourage them and speak with them – "Come on, let's show them that even with 10 players we can win" etc.

Sending off a player from the other team also requires mental preparation. You can not enter the trap of exaggerated confidence that – "We can sure win over 10 players!". Exploit the time until the player leaves the field to adjust your feelings and for rising the intensity of the game when it starts. Talk with the players around you and heighten motivation. **You have an advantage in numbers, but without hard teamwork, the advantage will be missed!**

Your injury during a game

Injury is part of the game and it is possible to cope with it, especially when someone else gets hurt. When you get injured this is a different story. When you are hurt, lying on the grass, struggling with pain and anger, your only goal is to return to the game as fast as possible and in full ability. Allow the medical staff to treat you, try to use that time to calm down. Take several deep breaths, relax your body, regulate your feelings and return to the game without a blow to your ability.

If you return to the game angry you won't be concentrated. You won't control your feelings you will very quickly find yourself out of the game, replaced by the coach after a mistake you have made or by the referee after you have committed a foul in an out-burst of your emotions.

Everyone (the fans, the press, the commentators, etc.) love when injured players continue to play. This is unreasonable. As a player you decide what is good for the team and what is best for your body. To continue playing when injured like everybody loves, but with half your ability, will only harm your team. If you feel that you are incapable to return to the game with your full ability and concentration, tell this to the coaching staff and let them take the right decision. If you are able to play with your full ability despite the pain you should check with the coaching staff that you are not damaging your body (may be you will finish the present game, but later you will miss 4 games because of injury complications). Let the doctor decide despite your will to continue with the game. As a professional player, you are not in a war ("I play till I can't move anymore"). You must assume that your body is your instrument and the profit of prolonging your presence on the field is in many cases smaller than the damage you might cause to yourself and the team.

Substituting a player

The pause in the game for the substitution of a player allows you several seconds of physical and mental rest. Your goal is to be fully concentrated when the game starts again. Quite a lot of goals are scored right after the substitution of a player. The new player is still not completely in the game (if he did not prepare mentally before the replacement). The rest of the players have not yet regained full and sufficient concentration and this combined with the new player and the change in the team formation leaves the players still not organized. And the result – mistakes and giving up goals. To prevent such situations it is your responsibility to be completely concentrated on performing your personal and team duties. You must check that the players around you are concentrated on the game. If you enter the game as a substitute remember that you do not have a minute to waste and you must join the game completely. You must be a part of the game immediately after its renewal. Only the right mental preparation together with your warm up will allow you to join the game immediately (see chapter 13).

Summary

- Be aware about special game conditions and take advantage of them.
- In the first minutes of the game and the second half the chances for mistakes are higher.
- Learn to regulate your stress and concentration to prevent you from making mistakes and to exploit the mistakes of the opponent.
- In the last minutes of the game and of the first half exhaustion and pressure impair your concentration and the chances for mistakes are higher. Keep your concentration and try to exploit the mistakes of the opposition.
- Halftime is important for rest and getting the instructions from the coach. Use the halftime for mental preparation as well.
- A great percentage of the goals are scored from set plays. Learn to take advantage of them and learn to prevent giving up goals from set plays with teamwork.
- The minutes after scoring or giving up a goal are minutes of lack of concentration and mistakes. Learn to keep your concentration in such situations and try to help your team mates preserve theirs too.
- It is possible with the right teamwork to take advantage of the minutes after scoring or giving up a goal to score again.

- Mistakes are part of the game and there isn't a player who does not make mistakes. How you interpret your mistakes can either ruin you or nurture you. Learn to disconnect from your mistakes and concentrate only on the present and not on what already has happened.
- When a teammate makes a mistake you should help him forget it and continue for ward. Anger, yelling, blames etc. will only lead the player to further concentrate on his mistake. An encouraging word about the future is much more efficient and allows disconnecting from the past and continuing with the game.
- Use the short pause in the game when an injured player receives treatment for "inject ing" mental encouragment.
- Penalties are kicked not only with the foot but also with the "head". Penalties are missed because of the "head". Learn to per form them correctly. The right mental work promises you won't miss!
- Sending off a player might lead to damage beyond his absence in the game. Loss of concentration might lead to defeat. Learn to regulate the anger and the emotions and learn to transform the loss of a player into a push of higher motivation.

- Sending off an opposing player does not automatically give you the advantage. This will happen only with hard work and increasing the motivation of the whole team.
- Learn to use injury for recovery and mental reinforcement. Control your emotions. When you return to the game you are stronger and in full control.
- Take decisions together with the team doctor about your ability to return to the game. Do not risk your future with worsening your injury. Anyway, an injured player in pain might cause his team a greater damage than the help of his presence on the field.

The Coach Box

With the right preparation it is possible to transform the special game conditions into situations to take advantage of. This requires preparation during training. Don't wait for the problems to occur and for your team to get goals from static situations. Train and be ready.

Training must include an unconditional demand from the players to control their emotions in every situation. **A player who cannot control his feelings in practice and loses concentration will certainly fail to control his emotions in the real game.**

Practicing how to play in the first and last minutes of the half and after scoring or giving up a goal, will prevent giving up unnecessary goals, will keep the team consolidated and the belief in the personal and team ability will lead to scoring.

Choosing the players for free kicks and penalties is not an

easy task. Pay attention that not necessarily those who are good during training will be good in the game too. During practice it is much easier to keep concentration and there is no pressure. A penalty kicker must prove himself in the game. Assist him in his mental preparation for performing penalties during practice. It is better to change the penalty kicker if he does not succeed in the game than to leave a player who does not miss in practice but during the game fails to succeed.

Chapter 23 – The goalkeeper is 80% of the team

I am not sure I agree with the title of the chapter, but this is the opinion of a great number of the people dealing with soccer. This chapter deals with the mental part of the goalkeeper's duties.

If you play as a goalkeeper this chapter is directed at you, however if you are not a goalkeeper do not skip it, because it certainly is directed at you too.

This chapter should help you recognize the special mental difficulties of the goalkeeper. Such understanding will allow you to assist the goalkeeper and will be of use for the entire team. From the other side a great part of the problems and solutions I offer to the goalkeeper are important for the rest of the players as well (how to look at mistakes, concentration, etc.).

Understanding the mental part of the goalkeeper's duties will make you a better goalkeeper and a better player if you are not a goalkeeper.

The goalkeeper's duties

We all agree that the role of the goalkeeper in modern soccer is very important, but very hard as well.

What exactly is hard in the role of the goalkeeper?

The need to keep maximum concentration for the whole game and the zero acceptability of mistakes.

Beyond the physical qualities of the goalkeeper (height, speed, jump, quickness etc.) he should also have mental abilities. Actually, a goalkeeper should have all the mental abilities of a soccer player, but on a higher level. Following are some of them:

- Concentration ability for a long time.
- Ability to be a leader of the defense.
- Ability to do disconnect from mistakes and concentrate only on the present.
- Ability to comprehend, analyze and take decision in minimum time.
- Reaction time as short as possible (it sounds like a physical quality, but it has an important mental element as well).
- Self-confidence and unshakable belief in ability.
- Maximum control over thoughts and feelings.

It does not matter how excellent the physical qualities of the goalkeeper are, without the appropriate mental ability he won't be a good goalkeeper. We all know goalkeepers who are capable of jumping and saving impossible balls, but give up a foolish goal minutes after it.

As with every player, but especially when we speak about the goalkeeper, the best expression of ability is **persistence.**

The goalkeeper must show maximum ability every game and throughout the game.

There are only a few goalkeepers like these!

The awareness about the coaching of goalkeepers has become greater, however even this special coaching usually consists of developing the physical qualities of the goalkeeper.

When practice is designed in a better way, the **goalkeeper** is dealing as well with decision making and learning from mistakes. The mental element in this case too, does not yet receive the emphasis it deserves.

If you are a goalkeeper and you decide to follow the way of training I offer in this book and especially in this chapter, I promise you will become a better goalkeeper!

We can see how difficult the mental work is for a goalkeeper in an "easy" game in which the opposing team almost did not threaten his goal. Even after such a game the goalkeeper is completely exhausted physically and mentally and often he is more tired than the players who ran for the whole game.

The need to keep concentration exhausts physically and mentally.

Some goalkeepers prefer games in which they are more involved (despite the chance of a goal), instead of a game in which they do not touch the ball. **It is much harder to keep full concentration, when you are not an active part of the game.**

If you are a goalkeeper, you must read several times the chapter dealing with concentration and you should practice what you read in your training and throughout the game.

The right mental work will significantly improve your ability. This chapter will provide you with several additional mental tools, but there is nothing better than practice.

Keeping concentration

In most games, you have relatively a lot of time when the ball is not near you, but on the other hand a change in this situation is extremely fast.

Do not lose concentration when the situation doesn't seem dangerous!

In the first stage if you want to achieve this you will need to recognize the factors that disturb your concentration during the game (be honest with yourself, you are not yet a perfect goalkeeper and there are things that hurt your concentration). Think and try to recognize the situations, which lower your concentration during the game. If your team has a goalkeeper coach, advise him too. It is extremely important to think together with the coach and discuss your concentration as well as the other weaknesses that you are aware of (advise him about the things you need to improve).

I do not want to give you the wrong ideas, but these are some examples of situations in which your concentration might be impaired:

- Curses from the crowd
- The weather
- A game in which you are not involved or several minutes you are away from the ball
- After giving up a goal
- After you made a mistake that did not lead to a goal
- After a defensive mistake
- When you are asked to coordinate offense
- TV cameras
- Your injury
- Night game. etc.

On one team the goalkeeper was one of the best goalkeepers in the league. He had difficulties concentrating when the coach asked him to organize the defense and be the leader of the teams defense **or in other words to shout. In such situations he did not succeed in shouting commands to the players and at the same time keeping full concentration**. The result was that either he didn't shout which left the defense disorganized or he shouted and as a consequence made mistakes because he lost his concentration.

Another goalkeeper had difficulty keeping concentration when he was not involved in the game. When he was in such situations after several minutes his mind began to fill with thoughts like – "What will happen when the ball approaches me the next time?", "What will happen when the opposition starts an attack?", "I am afraid that I won't see the next ball coming!" and more. As a consequence of the thoughts he suffered from lack of concentration in the game, when the ball finally reached him, he made a mistake.

The two goalkeepers were excellent, however we have seen that even the most famous goalkeepers in the world give up foolish goals at the same time they make miraculous saves. **It is all related to the difficulty to remain concentrated.**

In the cases I described, after the goalkeepers recognized there difficulties, they had the chance to practice it until they reached a state when it did not hurt their concentration anymore.

In the first case, the goalkeeper started shouting in training too. He simply practiced yelling!!! And he was aware of his concentration.

This goalkeeper learned to recognize when his concentration diminishes and immediately to take a deep breath, to tell himself a word like "**Concentrate!**" and to return to full concentration.

With practice the goalkeeper solved his problem and his shouting did no longer disturb his concentration. He became a real leader of the teams defense.

In the second case, the goalkeeper learned to control his

thoughts as described in the chapter about thought control (chapter 10). He learned to turn negative thoughts into positive and to use every thought for strengthening concentration and motivation. The goalkeeper worked hard in every training session and practiced thought control. In a relatively short time he established control over his thoughts with out dependence on game conditions.

In both cases the result of the improved concentration ability was performing less mistakes and a decline in the number of goals that were scored because of mistakes.

If you recognize the situations that impair your concentration, you can use what you read here to work and practice how to cope and prevent concentration impairment. However, you must be aware about the level of your concentration during the game and recognize immediately any decline in concentration.

With the help of deep breath, positive self-talk, thought control, key words (words you practiced in your visualization that return you immediately to concentration, see the chapter about visualization), body move (a fist, clapping hands, slapping yourself, etc. any move you practiced and it returns you to concentration), you will succeed in keeping maximum concentration throughout the whole game.

You must be constantly involved in the game to keep concentration even when your team is attacking all the time. **Do not disconnect from the game, follow the ball, live the game, be involved – shout or encourage from time to time, give instructions to the defense, move etc. Keep your concentration on the game and keep your eyes only on the field.**

Mistakes and receiving goals

Despite the effort you invest, and despite all you learned in this book, you will still eventually make a mistake. Sometimes only you know you did it and other times because of your mistake the opponent scores and everyone knows you did it. Sometimes even when your game is flawless your team will conceed goals anyway because of the mistakes of other players, etc. **The question is what happens after a mistake.**

Your first aim should be to disconnect from the goal you conceeded, to forget it and return to function in the present, in what is happening now on the field and not in what already has happened!

When you are busy thinking about the past: "Why didn't I advance towards the ball?", "I was able to prevent the goal", "I made a mistake again and the team got a goal", "Another mistake in defense and we gave up a goal". Any similar thought, but also thoughts about the future – "We will lose the game because of me", "This goal will cost us the championship", "What the coach thinks about me" – it always lead to the same result: **another mistake!**

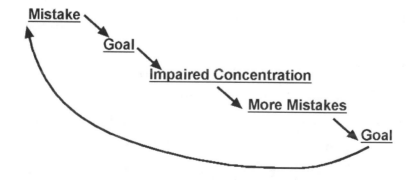

Another mistake goalkeepers make is to try and analyze the mistakes they made earlier during the game (what I did and what could I have done better). This analysis is certainly important, however this is not the time and place to think about it. You can discuss the analysis after the game. If you do it during the game you will not only impair your concentration but you will also increase the number of negative thoughts like - "Am I a goalkeeper at all", "A child would have done better…" and more.

Sometimes your teammates and the crowd "help" you blame yourself… and then you enter a tail-spin, in which mistakes hurt concentration, your lack of concentration hurts your self-confidence and belief in ability and this in turn hurts your ability. The final result is that you make a mistake again and the thoughts return again.

When we enter such a tail-spin it is very hard to escape from it. We all know goalkeepers who function without a flaw until they conceed a goal and then there is a drastic decline in their ability.

In order to escape this tail-spin it is important not to enter it at all. That's why you must stop yourself right after you made a mistake and if you will have to explain and be accountable for your actions to yourself and the team, you can do this after the game.

Your goal after making a mistake is to forget it, to return to full concentration and not to make additional mistakes.

So what can we do?

You made a mistake (a goal was scored or not), admit the mistake with raising your hand or any other move, and from this moment on **forget it and disconnect from it.**

You can do this with **quick body moves** like strong clapping of the hands (concentrate on the hands), **several jumps** (concentrate on the legs) or a short run. The movement is not important, choose any movement that suits you. **What is important is to concentrate on your body and the muscles you are activating**.

Take several deep breaths and with blowing the air out tell yourself – "With the air out I forget the mistake. My goal now is to be the best I can". **Encourage yourself with a couple of sentences like** – "Come on, get over it!", "I am a good goalie", "I believe in my ability", "I concentrate only on the game" etc.

If a goal is scored your aim is that until the game is restarted you will succeed in disconnecting from the goal and will be completely concentrated on what is happening now on the field!

If thoughts about the goal enter your mind later in the game, take a deep breath and tell yourself "Concentrate", "I believe in my ability" then continue with the game.

Reaction time

One of the important qualities of a goalkeeper is that his reaction time is as short as possible.

Reaction time depends mostly on physical abilities, but **it is also significantly influenced by mental factors as well.**

When you are concentrated, when you believe in your ability, when you are certain you are capable of stopping any ball – your reaction time gets shorter. **If you practice right in training on the physical side (jumping, changing direction etc.) the mental elements of your reaction time it will get shorter.**

In training and in the game you must be in a state that whatever action you perform (it does not matter if this is running for the ball, trying to stop a free kick or a penalty),

you perform it with complete belief in your ability to succeed!

When you have to stop a penalty you dive for the ball decisively and with intention to succeed and not just to fall on the ground!

If you have time before the execution of a free kick close your eyes for a few seconds and visualize how you stop the ball – your reaction time will shorten and the chances to succeed will grow.

Another way to shorten reaction time is to develop your ability to predict what the player is planning to do (where he is going to kick the ball, is he trying to shoot or is he going to pass the ball, etc.). **The difference between a beginner and an experienced goalkeeper is in the ability to predict the actions of the players**. Practicing this in training and with the help of video can assist you in compensating for the lack of experience. It will help you improve your ability and assess what is going to happen (pause the video right before the kick or the movement of the player and try to guess what he is going to do and then continue watching the video to see what the player actually does). It is recommended to work together with all the goalkeepers of the team. It is possible when watching a soccer game to practice your prediction abilities.

Taking decisions

The goalkeeper like any other player perceives information all the time. He analyzes the information, makes decisions and puts them into action. Even if you think that some of the actions are performed automatically they still follow the three stages. Every action you take is the result of a decision: leaving the goal, position, jumping, running, leaping, not going for the ball etc.

Your goal is to take the right decisions and execute them!

Actually, everything I have written in this book and in this chapter in particular is intended to help you make the right decisions. If you want to be better and make fewer mistakes you should start thinking in terms of decision-making.

When you are watching the video of your game you analyze the decisions you have taken. In training you practice making the right decisions and try to learn from mistakes.

In the game itself you make decisions at an incredible speed. You do not have time to think and analyze. If you want that your decision is not only fast but also correct, you must have the right practice of the physical and mental elements of the game. The use of video and working with a goalkeeper coach will advance you. Once more, you can stop the video before you see what the goalkeeper does and try to decide what he should have done, to continue with the video and see what actually he did and what was the result of his actions.

There are no shortcuts, but only hard work that will lead you to become a better goalkeeper!

Free kicks and penalties

In the previous chapter I wrote about the mental element in free kicks and taking of penalty kicks (from the shooter's perspective). Of course, the goalkeeper also has an important role and that the mental elements of his role in a free kick and the attempt to stop it are of major importance.

When you are preparing for a free kick your duties include – building the wall, organizing the defense and preparing yourself for the kick. **You must, with the coach's guidance, decide on the subjects you are responsible for and you must practice regularly building a wall and guiding the defense**. You must be concentrated on the kick. Too many goals are scored while the goalkeeper is shouting at his defenders and is not concentrated on the kick. Try to gather information about the regular kickers of the opposing team. This will help you prepare better. At the same time, you cannot try and guess what kind of kick it will be. You must wait for the execution of kick and only then decide what to do. Your main goal is remaining concentrated.

During a free kick you must concentrate just and only on the player behind the ball and the ball itself.

During this time you are not dealing with anger about the wall that did not listen to you, or about the player who committed the foul, and not with thoughts about what will happen if you fail to stop the ball. Full concentration and belief in your ability will increase your chances to stop the kick. If when you are jumping for the ball, or trying to reach a high ball, and in every other action you do your part with complete belief and determination your chances will grow.

The penalty is a special kind of a free kick. In the previous chapter I noted that penalties are missed because of the "head". Your role is to try and influence the mind of the kicker and to prepare your mind for stopping the ball.

When the referee whistles for a penalty your immediate goal is to prepare for its execution. You must disconnect from everything happening around you. Do not run to the referee to protest (it will not make any difference, let the other players argue with the referee), don't yell at the player who fouled etc.

From the moment a penalty is given and till the ball is kicked you must perform a "ritual" (a fixed series of actions) **that are aimed at increasing your concentration, to strengthen your self-confidence and the belief in your ability to stop the penalty.** Build yourself a series of movements or sentences you tell yourself, breathe deeply, kick the goalpost or adopt any other thing that helps you to disconnect and concentrate on the penalty.

When the kicker looks in your direction it is recommended to approach one of your teammates and exchange with him a few words (make the kicker wonder "What he told the goalkeeper?"). It is important to try and study the way the kicker takes penalties. Is he choosing a corner and then kicks the ball or he is making a diversion and looks which side you are jumping to. Accordingly you can prepare yourself. **Seconds before the penalty, rise your head, look in the eyes of the kicker saying "I will stop your ball you have no chance against me!", take a deep breath and try to stop the ball with determination.**

Of course, there is no use of mental work if you don't practice with persistence on stopping free kicks and penalties in training. You must practice the mental work in training!

It is a fact that stopping a penalty is more the result of a bad kick than a good goalkeeper reaction. Even though around the world there are goalkeepers whose saving percentages are relatively high. This fact only proves that the goalkeeper can do a lot.

Even to stop a ball, which is not a perfect kick you must have the right reaction. Practicing how to save penalties in training during the whole season (not only in the vicinity of a cup game) will make you a better goalkeeper.

Summary

- Understanding the goalkeeper's role and the mental elements of his position will advance not only the goalkeeper, but the rest of the players too.
- Learn to recognize what disturbs your concentration.
- Work in training on keeping your concentration in the situations that disturb you.
- Mistakes are part of the game. Practice your ability to disconnect from mistakes during training.
- The direst damage of making a mistake is sometimes much smaller than the damage you cause when you do not disconnect from the mistake.
- The correct mental preparation will shorten your reaction time.
- Mental work will improve your decision-making abilities.
- Perform every action with determination and complete belief in success!
- Free kicks including penalties require mental preparation and practice in training throughout the whole season.

The Coach Box

It is widely recognized that the contribution of a good goalkeeper to the team can be decisive for the team's success. Coaches not always transform the importance they give the goalkeeper's role into practice sessions.

Beyond the team practice, it is your duty to allow the goalkeeper to work with a specialist goalkeeper coach (or with you but separated from the team). The mental abilities of the goalkeeper should be developed as well – making decisions according to the game conditions, keeping concentration, etc. The right practice with the guidance of a goalkeeper trainer, video, analyzing decisions and learning from good plays and mistakes can push forward any goalkeeper. Goalies are famous with their eccentricities. If it does not hurt the team do not confront them.

Chapter 24 –
Weekly Program for Mental Training

The work on mental ability is done with the same importance as developing physical ability. The mental training program should be performed in the same way as you practice your body strength – day after day with the changes in training suited for the day of the game and the day after it.

Having a successful training program that will lead you to higher mental ability requires that the mental training becomes an integral part of your sportsman lifestyle. It must become a part of your sport practice. Only in this way mental training can be efficient and you will succeed to persevere with it for a long time.

The training program takes in to account that your game is on Saturday and so is your next game. The program accounts that you have a day without any physical training once a week (Monday). In case you play two games a week, perform the program from the beginning to end, but only shorten the times and adjust them to the time you actually have. If the team training program is changing for various reasons, change accordingly your mental practice program as well.

The training program should be performed throughout the whole active season, without any dependence on game results or your ability in a specific game. The training program must be performed in the same way before an "easy" game or a difficult game.

The last step (step 21) : Persistence

Remember that you cannot "cheat".
If you do not train the entire season, investing in
mental work only before the "game of
the season" won't be of any use!

Saturday – the end of the game, rest and recovery

Your only goal after the final whistle must be **rest and recovery, both physical and mental.**

On the first stage, you must disconnect from the game. What is important is to forget the game and leave it aside. You will have enough time to deal with it later, but not now. From your point the game is over. Now, you cannot change the result of the game and you cannot change the ability you showed in the game.

The score of the game should not determine your behavior. It is important to get used to practice without reflecting on the score. Of course, you are happy when you win and sad after a loss. However, practice must continue and the season is still long and if you want to be victorious for a long time you must continue your training.

It is recommended to decide on a steady behavior after a match, starting from the shower after the game until falling asleep. Your body must revive the energy resources that were used in the game and that is why you must eat and drink right and especially you must rest.

Your brain also needs a break. Perform at least twice a relaxation exercise with your favorite technique (chapter 8). Do this once after you finish eating at home and the second time before falling asleep (you will also guarantee a healthy sleep in this way). When playing out of town, use the time when traveling in the bus and later before falling asleep to perform a relaxation exercise.

Sunday – rest, recovery and analysis

Usually on this day there will be recovery training and sometimes also there will be a discussion over the previous game. You must try and adjust your way of training to what is accepted in the team. **On Sunday your main goal should be to continue with the rest and the recovery (both physical and mental) and at the same time to analyze the last game.**

In order to rest you perform the minimum necessary effort and try to rest as much as possible. It is important to continue following a proper diet.

You continue performing relaxation twice a day. Once after training and second time before going to sleep.

Find time during the day to sit alone and recapture your preparation for the game – how did you feel before the game, what were your feelings during the game and how did you play.

Beyond your personal ability it is important to think about your team role as well. You are trying to learn from the mistakes you made and from the plays you performed well. The emphasis is not only on your functioning during the game, but on the whole process from the preparation till the end of the game.

Be honest with yourself –
this is the only way to improve!
If similar work is done in the team take part in it.
If not, do it alone.

Monday – rest and the core of the analysis

Usually, this will be your free day from training. You are still trying to rest and recover. This day is intended for chores, treatments, etc, however it is for sure not intended for exerting effort, maybe some light exercise.

During the day you perform a relaxation exercise and one more before you go to sleep. You finish with the analysis of the last game so you can start preparing for next game from tomorrow. That's why it is important to continue analyzing the last game from your personal and team-role standpoints.

If you have the video of the game, it is very important to work with it. It is essential that the work with the video is done together with the coach and the team (even if it is done some other day), however if you can find the video it is worth it.

Even if you do not have the video, you are able to reconstruct the game from your memory, image after image. The emphasis should be on analyzing and working on the game. This requires from you to be concentrated and have a professional approach. Again, the emphasis is not only on the game itself, but also on the preparation for the game, on your feelings, etc.

**Do not enter the trap to judge yourself and the team only by the score.
We won – then everything was fine and you are great.
We lost – everything was bad and you are not worth anything!**

**This is a real trap that will not lead you anywhere.
Be realistic and critical. At the end you are supposed to end the analysis of the game with conclusions about your ability and preparation for the game.**

Look for your mistakes! Did you prepare in the best way possible? Did you follow the coach's instructions throughout the whole game? Did you feel positive and did you belief in your ability and in the team's ability during the whole game? Did you invest your maximum effort during the whole game? Did you perform your personal and team duties? Think over your decisions and actions during the game not only judging them by their results, but also according to the decision itself – was it right for the specific situation in the game.

At the end you must reach decisions about your functioning for the future. This will help you to continue to perform the good things and try and fix the mistakes and the things that didn't go well.

At the end of this stage you should leave the game behind you and disconnect yourself from it. If you have difficulties doing so and thoughts about the last game continue bothering you use a relaxation exercise to leave the game behind. **Be attentive to your thoughts, and on every thought connected to the last game that enters your mind, bring a new one about the coming game and your success in it.**

Tuesday – starting preparation for the next game

In some of the teams it is accepted to watch the video of the last game on this day. If your team does this, then you should per-form today what I wrote about the previous day. Anyway, even if you are dealing today with the last game, actually you are begin-ning to deal with the coming game as well.

The mental preparation for the next game is concentrated on collecting data, thinking, analysis, practice on the field, visualization, work under pressure, motivation and all the other subjects that are mentioned in this book.

The information you are gathering must be focused on the opposing team and on individual players, whom you are expected to face in the game. Get help from the coaching staff in collecting the data.

Additional information you need is the expectations of the coach for you in the coming game. If the coach does not announce the team line-up, you can still ask the coaches about their expectations from the player who will play in your position (ask them "If I am in the line-up for the next game, what do you expect from me?"). Analyze the information you have and think about your game style. During the day perform twice a short relaxation exercise and visualize after it. The following   chapter will provide you with examples of visualization exercises for different positions in the game.

Wednesday – preparation

Today begins your preparation for the coming game. Perform a relaxation exercise and visualize before you go out for practice.

In the training session you are trying to play and practice your playing style for the coming game. At this point usually the coaches also begin to talk about the opposing team and this is an opportunity to continue learning about the other team.

In the evening after you are back from training and after you have rested; work with visualization on the coming game.

Thursday – preparation, regulating stress

On Thursday you should already know if you are in the line-up or not. Anyway, your good practices can promise you a place in the line-up. That's why it is important to come prepared to training. At home before practice, visualize your playing style in **the next training session and in the coming game**. You regulate your motivation and stress to guarantee that you will have a successful practice.

In the changing room before going out for practice, try to find a couple of minutes to visualize and regulate your stress and motivation.

Usually in the evening the pressure begins to rise. The game is coming and the stress is rising. If you have some time after the training session you go to sleep, find some time and perform a relaxation exercise. Relaxation will help you lower the stress and will allow you to pass pleasantly the remaining time until you go to sleep. Anyway, it is important to have a good sleep and to be rested; this is the reason why it is important to lower the pressure. Perform a relaxation exercise in bed before you fall asleep (the goal is to fall asleep at the end of the exercise and usually this works well).

Friday – preparation, regulating stress

Usually the training on Friday morning is an easy one. Even if you won't usually practice your game style in this training session it is still important to visualize the coming game before the practice.

After the training, at home, find some time to work on tomorrow's game. This should be **mental work, in other words, you must summarize everything you know about the game tomorrow and you visualize.**

Perform a good visualization to regulate your motivation and your pressure to their optimal level, strengthen your belief in your personal and team ability.

During the day and in the evening the pressure is rising and you must regulate it. Take advantage of the stress and turn it into a challenge. Work according to the instructions of the book.

During the evening and before going to sleep, you perform a relaxation exercise.

Saturday Morning

In the hours before the game, the pressure is skyrocketing and this is normal. You must use the stress to your advantage. You can do this if you treat pressure as your friend. In this way it will not disturb you from showing your real ability and it will also push you forward, will help you prepare better for the game and will make you a better player. A real sportsman is assuming that the more stressed he feels this is a sign that the game is important for him and he will do everything to play better. However, a better game won't happen just like that. **You must work and prepare**. The whole week you prepared for the game and now you must perform the final adjustment

Build yourself a habit of everything you do on the day of the game – build a "ritual" (that will fit a home game and an away game when you are staying at a hotel with the team). Your goal is to regulate the stress to the level that matches your maximum ability.

Find the time to relax and visualize.

Saturday in the changing room

It is recommended to develop a habitual behavior for the changing room and for the warm-up before the game.

In the changing room, when you are dressed and ready, find 5 minutes for mental work. Perform a short relaxation exercise regulate the pressure to the desired level. Check your motivation. Verify that it is on the needed level. Regulate it if necessary. Visualize your game style. At the end of he visualization the belief in your personal and team ability grows and strengthens. Now you believe more in yourself, your self-confidence is stronger and you are ready to invest every necessary effort to have a good game and to win.

Warm-up on the field

Use the minutes of the physical warm-up for mental preparation as well. Check yourself again; are you ready for the game? Is your pressure level appropriate?

If you still feel too stressed, concentrate on your body feelings and perform a more intensive warm-up that will lower the pressure a bit. Follow the instructions you learned from the book.

> **This is the time for the final adjustment of your pressure level, self-confidence and motivation.**
> **This is the time to strengthen the belief in your ability.**

When the warm-up is about to end take several deep breaths and picture in your imagination a good play of yours from a successful game – a play that gave you joy and satisfaction. Feel the picture with all your senses. Take a deep breath and tell yourself – "Today I will also succeed showing my maximum ability". Take, now, another deep breath and think about your readiness for the game! You are certain that you will perform your personal and team duties from the opening whistle and until the end of the game! You are certain you will show your maximum ability!

The Game

In the game the mental work does not end.

You continue to integrate mental work throughout the game.

Turn into actions all you learned from the book.

Follow what is happening in your mind and on the field.

Change your game style if necessary.

**Take a deep breath every chance you have.
The deep breath gives you a
"motivational push".**

YOU WILL HAVE A GOOD GAME!!
GOOD LUCK

But remember:

Luck has nothing to do with your success!!!

Your success is the end result of your work

during the week and the whole season

on your mental ability!!!

Chapter 25 - Examples for visualization training

Visualization should be done according to the rules that were described in chapter 9. Before beginning to visualize you must relax for several minutes with the method you have chosen. In this chapter I will remind you of the methods of relaxation based on deep and regular breathing. The illustrations I bring you, are only examples. **What is important is the method**.

You decide what will be the content of every visualization.

You adjust yourself to fit the opponent,

your duty, the field, etc.

Remember, you are the director of the movie

playing in your mind, but you are also the actor.

Working with visualization will advance you

and will make you a better player.

Read the chapter several times and **learn how to start and finish visualization**. Read the instructions for your position in the game and change what ever is necessary. After studying the chapter you are ready to begin with the actual work.

You are the director. You give the instructions to yourself.

If you find it hard to work with visualization alone, it is advisable to speak to sport psychologist who will work with you to develop a tape and program for visualization work.

Before every visualization training

The following exercise must be performed before each visualization session. If you prefer other relaxation methods, choose one and only after performing it start the visualization.

- Choose a comfortable place to sit or lie down (not a bed and not a couch). It is best if the conditions are similar to the changing room, because you must visualize there as well.
- Close your eyes and concentrate on your breathing. Feel how the air enters and leaves. Try to clean your mind. You concentrate only on your breathing – a quiet, calm breathing.
- With eyes closed pass with your mind over all the parts of your body – head, eyes, neck, hands, stomach, legs. Check that nothing is tight – no muscle is tense.
- Your whole body is relaxed now and so is your mind.
- You concentrate only on the breathing…
- With your own pace, take 5 deep breaths. Breathe in the air slowly through your nose, fill your stomach with air, keep it for a few seconds and let the air leave very slowly without effort. Together with the air the pressure and stress also leave you.
- Take another 4 deep breaths…
- Concentrate on your regular breathing and start counting your breaths from 1 to 10 – calm and quiet breaths.
- Breathe 3 groups of 10 breaths like these…

Now you are ready to begin visualizing. Later you will find specific visualization exercises suited to your role on the field. Match them to your needs, learn and practice them.

The end of visualization

At the end of visualization you perform the following exercise:

- Let the images slowly disappear.
- Concentrate only on your breathing. Feel how the air enters and leaves your lungs.
- Your breath is calm and quiet.
- Imagine one of your good plays from a previous game. A play that gave you a good feeling – happiness, self-confidence and belief in your ability.
- Bring the image to your imagination together with all you felt when you made this play. Use all of your senses.
- Concentrate on the image and on your feelings and take a deep breath.
- In any situation in the game, when it is hard for you, take a deep breath and feel the emotion this play made you feel.
- Let the image slowly disperse.
- Concentrate on your breathing. With every breath you take your self-confidence is growing. So is the belief in your ability.
- With every breath out the pressure and stress leave you.
- Concentrate on your breathing… with every breath your body energizes and becomes stronger. You had a lot of good games and this game as well will be a good one. Concentrate on your breathing and count silently from 5 to 1. Your body fills with energy and becomes stronger with every number.
- You open slowly your eyes and remain seated for a few seconds.

- Choose a short slogan – a line from a poem, a short sentence, a small prayer or any thing else you think of (this can be also a simple sentence like "Come on, let's do it...") and tell it with complete belief in your ability. Add to it a body movement (clapping hands, fisting your hand, etc.)
- The slogan and the movement return you to full functioning and maximum ability. Do them also during the game. Now you are ready to play, you are ready to invest everything needed from you for winning the game...
Return slowly and gradually to your normal functioning.

Working with visualization

After you have finished with the relaxation prior to visualization you are ready to begin.

- Visualization is done with closed eyes.
- Everything happens at present, It's happening right now .
- You are playing in this moment.
- You integrate into visualization as many senses as possible.
- The actions are done with their regular speed and intensity.
- You always succeed with your actions in visualization.
- You return several times over the same image or action.

Visualization exercise for a goalkeeper

- **In the beginning relax as described in the beginning of the chapter.** Begin working with visualization after several minutes of relaxation…

- It happens to you right now – you are in the warm-up before the game. See yourself and the rest of the players from the team. Remember a good game you played, a game with perfect ability. Feel the way you felt in this game. You have full belief in your ability; you are going to have a good game.

- You are playing now, see yourself in control of the penalty area, jumping for high balls and saving them. Feel the movements you make, hear your shouting. You are yelling "Mine!" and holding the ball. See yourself again and again go out and intercept the ball. Work on the images in your mind.

- Let the picture slowly disperse and concentrate on your breathing. Feel the air enter and leave your body…your breath is calm and quiet…you are completely concentrated on your breath…

- You are now in the game. It happens to you right now. You are the leader of the defense and you are the "king" of the penalty area. See yourself guide the defense. Hear yourself. The defenders believe in you. You are shouting, encouraging, reprimanding and always positive. You remain concentrated on the game and read its development. Return again and again over the images and the voices of your work as a leader of the defense.

- Let the images slowly disappear and concentrate on your breathing. Feel the air enter and leave your body…your breath is calm and quiet...you are completely concentrated on your breath...

- It happens to you right now. You are in the game. Bring to your imagination images of game situations inside your penalty area (shots and crosses). See yourself. Feel your movement, see yourself jump with confidence for every ball and intercepting it. Every jump for the ball you take is guided by your full belief in your ability to stop the ball. There is not a ball you can't stop. Work with your imagination on shots and crosses and how you stop them in different game situations and free kicks. See the ball, feel the movements you make. This happens to you right now...

- Let the images slowly disappear and concentrate on your breathing. Feel the air enter and leave your body...your breath is calm and quiet...you are completely concentrated on your breath...

- You are now in the game. This is happening to you right now. You are completely concentrated on the game; nothing can distract your attention. See yourself and feel your movements. You are heading towards an opponent player. You leap from where you are standing like a rocket. You are fast, determined and completely sure in your ability to reach the ball first and save it without a foul... See yourself again and again in different situations one on one. You save every ball, you are always faster.

- Let the images slowly disappear...

- **End the exercise according to the instructions in the beginning of the chapter.**

Visualization exercise for a defender

This exercise is for any defensive player. Front and back sweepers have a bit different duties, so you can adjust the exercise to fit your role in the game.

- **Perform a relaxation exercise before visualization as described in the beginning of the chapter**. Transfer to visualization after several minutes of relaxation...

- It happens to you right now. You are warming up before the game. See yourself together with the other players from the team. Remember a good game you had – a game of perfect ability...feel now as you felt in this game. Use all your senses. You have full belief in your ability, you will have a good game.

- Now you are in the game. It happens to you right now. See yourself and feel the movements you make. You are heading for the player with the ball. You approach him with determination and with complete self-confidence that you will take the ball successfully from him without a foul...See the image again and again.

- Let the images slowly disappear and concentrate on your breathing. Feel the air enter and leave your body...your breathing is calm and quiet...you are completely concen trated on your breath...

- You are in the in the game now. It happens to you right now. See yourself and feel the movements you make. You see yourself rise for a high ball. You jump towards the ball with determination with complete belief you will reach it. See yourself on different positions on the field jump for a ball, feel your movement. See yourself against an oppo- sing player – you are faster than he is and you clear the ball away with a precise pass.

- Let the images slowly disappear and concentrate on your breathing. Feel how the air enters and leaves you...your breath is calm and quiet...you are com pletely concentrated on your breath...

- You are playing now. It happens to you right now. See yourself and feel your movements. See yourself close to an opposing player when the other team is attacking. See yourself again and again in different positions on the field, faster than the opponent, reading correctly his passes and intercepting the ball. See yourself...

- See yourself dealing with high balls, You stay close to a player and you are not looking for the ball. You concentrate on the player you are marking! You ad-vance towards the player and if the ball comes in your direction you take it. See yourself follow and guard an opposing player.

- Let the images slowly disappear and concentrate on your breathing. Feel the air enter and leave your body...your breath is calm and quiet...you are com pletely concentrated on your breath...

- You are now in the game. This happens to you right now. See yourself and feel the movements you make. See yourself join the offense. You are advanc-ing with the ball along the sideline, raise your head and pass the ball precisely. See yourself again and again break forward and pass the ball precisely.

- See yourself join the offense and pass the ball in dif-ferent situations on the field.

- See yourself return with determination to defense.
- Let the images slowly disappear and concentrate on your breathing. Feel the air enter and leave your body…your breath is calm and quiet…you are com pletely concentrated on your breath…
- **End the exercise according to the instructions from the beginning of the chapter**.

Visualization exercise for a midfielder

Midfielders have various duties with their emphasis changing from offense to defense. When visualizing pay attention to your duties.

- **Perform a relaxation exercise before visualization as described in the beginning of the chapter**. Transfer to visualization after several minutes of relaxation…
- This happens to you right now. You are warming up before the game. See yourself together with the rest of the team. Remember a good game you had – a game of perfect ability…feel now as you felt in that game. Use all your senses. You have full belief in your ability and will have a good game.
- It happens to you right now. You are in the game. See yourself help the defense, head for the ball with determi nation, take it away from an opposing player without a foul. See yourself and feel your movements. See yourself again and again win a ball in different places on the field.
- You are on the ball now. It happens to you in this moment. See yourself raise your head and find a precise pass for a goal. See yourself and feel the movement. See yourself pass the ball precisely again and again.

- Let the images slowly disappear and concentrate on your breathing. Feel the air enter and leave your body...your breath is calm and quiet...you are completely concentrated on your breath...
- It happens to you right now. You are on the field. See yourself join an attack. Perform a give and go, shoot and score. See yourself again and again perform a give and go, shoot and score.
- It happens to you right now. See yourself and feel the movement. See yourself receive a ball in the penalty area, shoot and score. See yourself again and again shoot and score from different places in the penalty area.
- Let the images slowly disappear and concentrate on your breathing. Feel the air enter and leave your body...your breath is calm and quiet...you are completely concentrated on your breath...
- You are now in the game. It happens to you in this moment. See yourself take a free kick. See yourself and feel the movement from different static positions kicking the ball precisely and scoring. See yourself pass a good ball to a teammate who converts it into a goal. See yourself do this several times.
- You are now in the game. It happens to you right now. See yourself take a good position, run and jump for a header.

You are rising with determination and with complete belief that you will hit the ball successfully. You hit it and score. See yourself and feel the movements you make. See yourself in different positions on the field jump and head the ball successfully.

- Let the images slowly disappear and concentrate on your breathing. Feel the air enter and leave your body...your breath is calm and quiet...you are completely concentrat ed on your breath...
- This happens to you right now. You are in the game. See yourself with the ball and feel your movements. You are with the ball and the opponent players pressure you. They jump over you... See yourself again and again with out panic, make a good move and pass the ball safely. See yourself several times, the opponent players are try ing to pressure you. You are calm and you perform a good move passing the ball accurately...
- Let the images slowly disappear and concentrate on your breathing. Feel the air enter and leave your body...your breath is calm and quiet...you are completely concentrat-ed on your breath...
- **Finish the exercise according to the instructions from the beginning of the chapter**.

Visualization instructions for an offensive player

- **Perform a relaxation exercise before visualization as described in the beginning of the chapter**. Transfer to visualization after several minutes of relaxation...
- It happens to you right now. You are warming up before the game. See yourself together with the rest of the team. Remember a good game you had. Use all your senses. This is a game of perfect ability... Feel now as you felt in that game. You have complete belief in your ability and you will have a good game.
- This is happening to you right now. You are in the game.

See yourself and feel your movements. You are in attack. Make a give and go, shoot and score. See yourself perform a give and go, shoot and score several times...

- It happens to you right now. See yourself and feel the movements. See yourself receive the ball in the penalty area, shoot and score. See yourself again and again in different places in the penalty area shoot and score...

- Let the images slowly disappear and concentrate on your breathing. Feel the air enter and leave your body...your breath is calm and quiet...you are completely concentrated on your breath...

- You are now in the game. This is happening to you right now. See yourself take good position, run and jump for the ball. You are rising with determination and with full belief that you will head the ball successfully. You hit it and score. See yourself and feel your movements. See yourself jump and head successfully in different positions on the field...

- It happens to you right now. See yourself and feel the movement. You are helping the defense. Saving balls, reading the game correctly and preventing passes. You approach an opposing player and steal the ball from him without a foul. You stop a fast attack, take control of the ball and make a good pass. See yourself...

- Let the images slowly disappear and concentrate on your breathing. Feel the air enter and leave your body...your breath is calm and quiet...you are completely concentrated on your breath...

- You are now in the game. It happens to you right now. The ball is at your feet, see yourself and feel the move ment. You advance with the ball with determination, dummy past a defender, shoot with determination and score. See yourself again and again, dribble with the ball, past players, shoot and score...feel the movements...

- See yourself and feel your movements. You advance with the ball, past defenders and send an exact pass to a teammate. See yourself, again and again from different positions on the field, dribble with the ball and make a good pass...

- It happens to you right now. You are in the game. See yourself with the ball and feel your movements. You are dribbling with the ball and the opposing players pressure you, they jump over you... See yourself again and again, you are not tense, you make a good move and find a safe pass. See yourself several times with the opposing players trying to steal the ball from you. You are not pressured; you make a good move and send a good pass...

- Let the images slowly disappear and concentrate on your breathing. Feel the air enter and leave your body...your breath is calm and quiet...you are completely concentrated on your breath...

- **Finish the exercise according to the instructions from the beginning of the chapter.**

Visualization exercise for a game on a field, on which you do not succeed.

Every player and every team always have a certain stadium on which they do not play well. **When you believe in this, the chances are that your next game on this field won't be a good one too.** To prevent this happen, **add to the beginning**

of your visualization exercise the following element:

- You are now in the game. This is happening to you right now.
- See yourself with the rest of the team enter the field for a warm-up.
- Bring to your imagination an image of the stadium. Begin looking from above the lights, the roof, the crowd and the grass.
- On this grass you are going to have a good game – you and the entire team.
- Bring to your imagination good plays from your previous games. See the images, feel the movements and experience your great satisfaction. You will make such plays today as well on this field.
- It happens to you right now. See yourself perform good defensive and offensive plays on this field. See yourself, again and again…
- Let the images slowly disappear and concentrate on your breathing. Feel the air enter and leave your body…your breath is calm and quiet…you are completely concentrated on your breath…
- **Continue with the visualization exercise matching your team role.**

Visualization exercise for a game directly transmitted on TV

Some of the players do not succeed in showing their full ability in games that are directly transmitted on TV. The lights, the TV cameras around the field, the press coverage – all these impair concentration and hurt the ability of the players.

Add to the beginning of your visualization exercise the following element:

- It happens to you right now. You are in the game.
- See yourself enter the field for a warm-up. See the TV cameras standing around. The lights are lit.
- Tell to yourself "I will have a good game today", "The stage is ready for my best play". Tell this several times with complete belief...
- Bring to your imagination good plays from your previous games, see yourself, feel the movements you did then and experience the great satisfaction of your success.
- This game too, on this field, with the TV cameras around you will make good plays. See yourself. You are in the game now. It happens to you right now. You are aware about the presence of the cameras, but you do not see them, they do not bother you. You are entirely concentrating on the game and you make good plays. You succeed with every play you make.
- See yourself again and again, feel the movements. You perform good plays...you had many good games before and this game too will be a good one too...
- Let the images slowly disappear and concentrate on your breathing. Feel the air enter and leave your body...your breath is calm and quiet...you are completely concentrated on your breath...
- **Continue with the matching visualization exercise**.

Visualization exercise for a game with a huge audience

Part of the players do not succeed in showing their full potential in games with huge audiences.

To prevent this, add the following exercise to the beginning of the visualization session:

- It is happening to you right now. You see yourself enter the field for a warm-up.
- See the crowd filling the stadium.
- Listen to the thunder of the crowd.
- You are going to have a good game despite this crowd.
- Tell yourself several times with full belief: "I will have a good game despite this crowd...".
- This is happening to you right now. You are just before the opening whistle of the game. Look at the crowd for the last time. Concentrate on the colors. You see only colors.
- Very slowly take down your eyes and look at the grass. Your concentration transfers from the stadium to the grass. On this grass you will have a good game. You are disconnecting from the crowd, you are only in the game. This happens to you right now. See yourself and feel the movements you make. You make good plays and you succeed in every pass and tackle you make.
- See yourself from different positions on the field performing good skills time after time.
- Let the images slowly disappear and concentrate on your breathing. Feel the air enter and leave your body...your breath is calm and quiet...you are completely concentrated on your breathing...
- **Continue with the visualization exercise visualizing your team role.**

Visualization will advance you.
Visualization is pleasant.
There is no sweat in visualization
so there is no reason not to practice it!

REMEMBER!
VISUALIZING SUCCESS
SHORTENS THE WAY TO SUCCESS!

Chapter 26 – The Final Whistle

In the beginning of the book I promised you that if you adopt
even a small part of the ideas mentioned in the book –
you will improve in everything you do.
Psychology cannot give you magic injection that will turn
you in a moment to a better player.
Psychology offers you only a working program, which when
followed, without a doubt will make you a better player.
Do not expect immediate change,
follow the program and the change will come.

You read the 21 steps that will lead you from
the place you stand now to new highs.
However, nobody else can climb instead of you.
This is a journey you must do alone!
These are the steps you should follow without a break –
all along your soccer career!

If you have questions on sport psychology or you want to know more about any of the subjects in this book you can send me an email: rafisrr@isdn.net.il

Additional books that helped me to write this book and can help you too:

1. Beswick, B .2001.**Focused for Soccer**.
   Champaign, IL. Human Kinetics.
2. Benson, H.1975. **The Relaxation Response**.
   New York. Morrow.
3. Cabrini, M .1999. **The Psychology of Soccer**.
   Spring City, PA, Reedswain.
4. Goldberg, A.1997.**Playing Out of Your Mind**.
   Spring City, PA, Reedswain.
5. Goldberg, A, S.1997.**Sport Slump Busting**.
   Champaign, IL.Human Kinetics.
6. Jackson, P, Delehanty, H. 1995. **Sacred Hoops**.
   New York. Hyperion.
7. Loehr, E, J.1993. **Toughness Training for Life**.
   New York. Dutton.
8. Porter, K. Foster, J.1986. **The Mental Athlete**.
   New York. Ballantine Books.
9. Syer, J. Connolly, C.1984. **Sporting Body Sporting Mind**. London. Sport Pages.
10. Syer, J. Connolly, C.1991. **Think to Win**.
    London. Simon&Schuster
11. Terry, P. 1989. **The Winning Mind**.
    Northamptonshire. Thorsons Publishing Group.
12. Weinberg,R,S. Gould, D.1995.**Sport and Exercise Psychology**. Champaign, IL.Human Kinetics.

The Internet is a good place to find additional sport psychology resources. You can start from:

http://www.aaasponline.org

For books and videos on soccer go-to:

http://www.reedswain.com/default.htm

Also available from Reedswain:

Also available from Reedswain: